Always an Academic Immigrant

Always an Academic Immigrant

A Collective Memoir

DAFNA LEMISH

Rutgers University Press
New Brunswick, Camden, and Newark, New Jersey
London and Oxford

Rutgers University Press is a department of Rutgers, The State University of New Jersey, one of the leading public research universities in the nation. By publishing worldwide, it furthers the University's mission of dedication to excellence in teaching, scholarship, research, and clinical care.

Library of Congress Cataloging-in-Publication Data

Names: Lemish, Dafna, 1951– author.
Title: Always an academic immigrant : a collective memoir / Dafna Lemish.
Description: New Brunswick : Rutgers University Press, [2025] | Includes index.
Identifiers: LCCN 2024041343 | ISBN 9781978843615 (paperback) | ISBN 9781978843622 (hardcover) | ISBN 9781978843639 (epub)
Subjects: LCSH: Immigrants—Education, Higher—Cross-cultural studies. | Immigrants in higher education—Cross-cultural studies. | Immigrant college teachers—Cross-cultural studies. | Immigrants—Biography. | Universities and colleges—Employees—Social conditions—Cross-cultural studies.
Classification: LCC LC3727 .L46 2025 | DDC 378.1/55—dc23/eng/20241226
LC record available at https://lccn.loc.gov/2024041343

A British Cataloging-in-Publication record for this book is available from the British Library.

Copyright © 2025 by Dafna Lemish
All rights reserved

No part of this book may be reproduced or utilized in any form or by any means, electronic or mechanical, or by any information storage and retrieval system, without written permission from the publisher. Please contact Rutgers University Press, 106 Somerset Street, New Brunswick, NJ 08901. The only exception to this prohibition is "fair use" as defined by U.S. copyright law.

References to internet websites (URLs) were accurate at the time of writing. Neither the author nor Rutgers University Press is responsible for URLs that may have expired or changed since the manuscript was prepared.

♾ The paper used in this publication meets the requirements of the American National Standard for Information Sciences—Permanence of Paper for Printed Library Materials, ANSI Z39.48-1992.

rutgersuniversitypress.org

For my beloved mother Chaya Barkai (1925-2016), who was deeply saddened when we immigrated, and to my granddaughters Lia, Milly, and Rona (and their future siblings and cousins), who I hope will reap the benefits of that journey.

Contents

1	The Journey: Why This Book?	1
2	The Seeds: Do Childhood Experiences Prepare for Immigration?	23
3	The Voyage: What Are the Reasons for Immigration?	37
4	The Challenges: Why Is Immigration So Difficult?	58
5	The Benefits: What Are These Academics Uniquely Contributing?	85
6	The Home: Where Is Home for Academic Immigrants?	106
7	The Bridge: What Keeps Immigrants Connected?	126
8	The Return: Would They Consider Going Back?	143
9	The Support: What Can Be Done to Help Academic Immigrants?	156
	Postscript: Once an Immigrant, Always an Immigrant	164
	Notes	169
	Index	177

Always an Academic Immigrant

1
The Journey

Why This Book?

"It Has a Healing Effect on Me"

This project was born out of my personal journey. I like to fondly call it my "3Ps" exploration: personal-professional-political. At the age of fifty-eight, amid a flourishing career in Israel, as a tenured full professor at the Department of Communication at Tel Aviv University, I decided to advance my career path in academic administration in the United States.

In concrete terms, I had just signed a three-year contract to serve as chair of the Department of Radio and TV at Southern Illinois University in Carbondale, Illinois. A place I had not even heard of until a few months earlier. Yet, here we were, Peter (my husband and partner for close to half a century now) and I, flying back to Israel to pack up the materials of our lives there. But all of this is not quite so simple, as we found in the following days, months, and years.

First, packing involved making tens of immediate decisions about minutiae—what is to be shipped, stored, donated, and discarded. I sifted through my office drawers for my most dear memorabilia. I selected some of my treasured decorations collected over decades of traveling the world for conferences and academic engagement. I sorted through boxes of papers and old research data. These mini decisions were a small part of this huge unknown: as the past passed through me, I also began to wonder about what future investigative and administrative endeavors would evolve with my move to America. How would my professional trajectory fare?

Second, though I explained this decision to myself and others in Israel as "I decided to extend my stay in the United States following a sabbatical," in reality, reaching and implementing this decision were much more complicated and challenging than we had anticipated. Indeed, there was something much deeper and transformative going on in our decision to "extend our sabbatical," and everyone understood that. It happened at the age of fifty-eight, but it really was a culmination of a lifelong process, encapsulated in the "3Ps."

Third, in reality, in my case as well as with so many of the voices of immigrants whose stories I will share with you, the "professional," the "personal," and, in my case, the "political" are entwined cornucopia. Unwinding, probing, reflecting upon, and reinterpreting them is a complex, challenging emotional endeavor. Put simply, immigration is complicated, frightening and exciting, destabilizing and reinvigorating, painful and liberating.

My Personal desire to be close to my children (which expanded later with the birth of our granddaughters) took me away at the same time from everyone else meaningful to me—my mother, siblings and their families, extended family members, friends, colleagues, and former students. I felt an enormous emotional push and pull. There was longing, the power of nostalgia, lost social capital, challenges imposed by my Israeli identity . . . and there was the pain I know I caused my mother, the silence in reunions in Israel of my loved ones avoiding putting into words what they probably thought of our "betrayal" to our still young country.

At times like this, I couldn't avoid thinking of the infamous term targeting people like myself who had left Israel as *neh'folet shel neh'moshut* (translated from Hebrew as roughly to "cowardly dropouts"), once uttered by later assassinated Prime Minister Itzhak Rabin in a 1976 television interview. It is no accident that the word "immigrate to Israel" translates into Hebrew as *aliya*, ascending, while the word for emigration away from Israel is called *yerida*, descending. The implied meaning is that when you leave the country—which in my case is not "just" any country, but "the promised land"—your Israeliness diminishes, your value as a Jew loyal to the tradition and legacy of the Jewish people diminishes, your commitment to your people and the ideals of the country diminishes. In other words, you are a disgrace and your self-image as a Jew should be irreparably harmed.

My Professional group of motivations led me to seek a lateral move—looking again for a chair position that would allow me to learn the ins and outs of American academia as well as institutional structures and expectations. At the same time, I was suddenly available for an endless parade of keynote invitations and enjoyed traveling the country, meeting colleagues and students, widening my networks in multiple ways, and attending my associations' conferences without the debilitating jetlag.

My Political group of reasons is probably the most difficult to admit and to process. The decline of Israeli democracy and the crisis brought about by the ongoing occupation of territories since the 1967 Six-Day War and the conflict with the Palestinian people and the Arab world haunted and engaged our family's life for decades before our making the decision to leave. The trend seemed irreversible already then. The immorality of continuing to live and support via our taxes governmental policies we opposed so strongly, the anxiety over the possibility of our grandchildren being raised to fight another senseless war, and of all of us forever living with the post-traumatic stress disorder induced by the life under constant threats of an unresolved conflict led us to that breaking point—or perhaps epiphany moment, depending on the eyes of the beholder.

I attribute that moment of my momentous decision to the night President Barack Obama was elected. We had a viewing party at our small, rented apartment in Brookline, near Boston, where we were living at the time, walking distance from the Center for Media and Child Health, affiliated with Harvard Medical School and Boston Children's Hospital, where I was spending my sabbatical. Two of my former Ph.D. students who happened to be in that area on postdoctoral fellowships joined us for this monumental event. When the night was over, I told Peter, who had been light-years ahead of me in his analysis of the decline of democracy in Israel and ready to leave years earlier, that OK, I am ready to stay here. A country that is, seemingly, so progressive, so willing to move forward to correct past traumas and wrongdoing—this is the country where I want to live (naïve, right? Little did we know then how the pendulum of history would swing again). Thus, another P was added to my 3Ps, now: personal, professional, political, and presidential.

And so, we stayed. That was fourteen years ago. It feels like a lifetime—filled with many opportunities, advancements, and, yes, oh so many challenges.

The Roots

Throughout my career, I've been fostering a hunch that many academics, myself included, study topics for which they have not only a personal interest but also some emotional or mental need to explore and/or perhaps an opportunity to rework trauma, pleasure, or an unresolved yearning. This book is no different. My colleague's "The personal is political is intellectual" serves me well here, too.[1]

For example, one colleague who is an adamant news consumer studies news; another loves soap operas and investigates them; and a colleague who is very involved with the political left of Israel studied the news coverage of the Israeli-Palestinian conflict. Similarly, I recently encountered an article about academic fraudsters who cheat in their own research and at the same time publish scholarly work on cheating in academic work.[2]

With time, I also noticed how my students used their seminar papers and term projects to work through their personal issues. In my gender classes, for example, I had students struggling with eating disorders write their papers on gender representations in the media and the development of a negative body image. Others studied the role of the internet in coming out as gay or queer, the process of integrating as an immigrant to a host country, and what it is like to receive mental health support. In my children and media courses, students who were young parents chose to write about parenting styles and the dilemma of using media at the early ages of their baby or toddler, or working through the disagreements between two parents.

My own career path followed my awakening to a feminist sensibility as I became a mother of three children. When at the age of not quite four our elder son was joined by a baby brother, I studied the processes of socialization of babies to television viewing during my postdoctoral fellowship with CRITC (The Center for Research on the Influences of Television on Children, at the University of Kansas at Lawrence).[3] When our daughter, who joined her brothers five years later, was a kindergartner, I studied kindergartners' understanding of the medium of TV while serving as a visiting scholar at the Annenberg

School for Communication (University of Pennsylvania).[4] And when she moved into her tween years and was consumed by the Spice Girls pop group, I went ahead and tried to understand their spell on girls.[5] The list goes on. Indeed, now as a grandmother, I am studying the role of grandparents in mediating their grandchildren's media use.[6] So yes, dear reader, one may wonder whether I will be studying media in retirement homes when the time comes. Maybe.

I always wanted to be a journalist, the kind that travels the world and meets unfamiliar cultures and people. I imagined myself working for *National Geographic* or a similar outlet. I envisioned myself as a journalist—traveling the world, meeting and talking to people, and writing. Life and serendipity took me on a seemingly very different route and I found myself in academia. However, through the years I discovered that my passion for listening to people makes a great method of inquiry. So as an academic, I ended up traveling a lot, developing the method of interviewing, and writing, writing, writing...

Moving more closely to the story of how this book evolved, I can say that I have always been fascinated by how inner processes of identity reflections, as well as wondering and struggles that underlie them, are often clarified through academic investigation. One of my former Ph.D. student who studies gays' lived experiences, strongly identifies with bell hooks, who confessed, "I came to theory because I was hurting. I came to theory desperate, wanting to comprehend. [...] Most importantly, I wanted to make the hurt go away, I saw in theory then a location for healing."[7] Maybe, indeed, this book has emerged out of a process of healing.

More specifically, the rough idea for the investigation presented in this book was "born" as I traveled back home to Israel from our sabbatical home in Boston (wondering about the concept of home and whether it would change) and fated to face my family and colleagues, and most importantly, my beloved elderly mother, and relate our decision to "extend our stay in the United States." Yet, instead of pondering what lay ahead, I chose to undertake the mindless job of creating the list of index words for the proofs of the book I just completed on gender representations in children's media during the long plane trip across the Atlantic Ocean.[8] However, subconsciously, as the flight continued, my heart was already in the future of my immigration story and my burning desire was to move forward with this new project, now before you. I remember getting up from my seat in the dark of the cabin, digging through the storage area for my backpack, pulling out my laptop, and sitting down to design this project. That was in 2010. I wrote these lines in 2024. It did not come easily. I ended up with nine more other books published between then and now.[9]

The Study

Like myself, over a quarter of the full-time faculty in my School of Communication and Information at Rutgers University are academic immigrants. At the College of Mass Communication and Media Arts at Southern Illinois University, my previous institution, it was close to a fifth of all full-time faculty.

Academic immigrants in many departments constitute a significant part of the full-time faculty, yet they barely receive the attention they deserve as a unique population. As I was navigating my own experience as an immigrant, I became particularly interested in this topic, both personally and intellectually.

Throughout, I have found myself continually reflecting on similarities and differences between my different academic worlds—the one I left behind and the one I joined here. I wondered about my many immigrant colleagues: Do they, too, feel they are living double lives? While we believe that we bring unique value to our "host" institutions, do our colleagues as well as leaders of our institutions understand the challenges we confront in this transition, and for years to come? Do they value and foster the sharing of our differing perspectives? The more I reflected on these and other questions, the more eager I became to hear the personal stories and reflections of other academic immigrants working in higher education. Admittedly, initially, this was a form of self-therapy. Further on, as a scholar who investigates the media's role in immigrant families' lives, among other phenomena, I utilized my deep intellectual interests and experience to advance this research project.

Much has been written about international scholars from a transactional perspective, particularly about the flows of knowledge they stimulate, their innovative contributions, and the value they bring to the economy and national development. More specifically, a recent survey of the policy motivations for the internationalization of higher institutions in the United States found that the three most common reasons cited were to prepare students for a global era (70 percent); to diversify students, faculty, and staff (64 percent); and to attract prospective students (45 percent).[10]

The growing mobility of academic migrants must be interpreted more broadly as part of this trend toward the internationalization of institutions of higher education as well as the capitalist discourse of globalization more generally.[11] The patterns of such mobility are determined by a host of political, economic, and social forces. Additionally, they are constrained by a variety of considerations related to human diversity including race, gender, religion, and nationality.[12] As a result, the terminology of "brain drain" and "brain gain" that has dominated such analysis has been challenged more recently, and a postcolonial lens has been applied by some researchers and observers to academic mobility and the knowledge economy.[13]

For example, the fluctuations in enrollment of international students in American universities have been explained by a variety of reasons, including an effort by the countries of origin of these potential students to mitigate the potential "brain drain" of their bright and promising researchers from the local economy and nation building. The following anecdote shares a different approach. Recently I met with several leaders from a university in Malaysia seeking collaborations with U.S. universities that will accept their students' credits and allow them to graduate with an American degree. When I asked how many current students return to Malaysia and whether there is concern about "brain drain," they responded that their commitment is first of all to the success of their students, and in any event, their country cannot absorb all the graduates. In contrast, other countries guarantee the return of their citizens after studying abroad by tying sponsorship to commitments to return and work in the home country.

One of the areas of research within this body of scholarship, which has received relatively limited attention until recently, focuses on the lived experiences of academic immigrants.[14] Indeed, there are but a few published collections of personal narratives of faculty and students.[15] This noted, what I set out to do was quite simply to hear academic immigrants' personal stories, lived experiences, issues with which they struggle, and academic contributions of which they are most proud. Additionally, I wanted to learn what they define as "home"; what they miss from their previous lives; what they retain of their cultural roots; and whether and if so are they considering a return to their country of origin on retirement and/or to be buried or cremated close to family. Above all, I wanted to humanize reporting about them while more specifically learning about their integration experiences in the higher education institutions that hosted them. Simultaneously, I also wanted to be able to reflect on these narratives on a more macro level, beyond the individual stories, to find the commonalities and thematic threads that tie their experiences together to each other. I wanted to be able to understand the phenomena in question beyond the personalized case and my own experience.

As someone raised in Israel to reject the mythology of the cursed "Wandering Jew," doomed to travel the earth, be uprooted until the Second Coming, and the culturally mixed bag of stereotypes that emerged over centuries in anti-Semite Europe, I am particularly sensitive to the concept of "the Wandering Scholar"; that is, an academic who assumes a transnational identity and cosmopolitan positioning, occupying an "in-between" cultural space that frees the individual from the geo-political boundaries of nation-states.[16] However, such a view also presumes a lack of permanency and roots. Further, it invites suspicions over loyalty and trust. Alternatively, a referent to academic mobility seems to be an ambiguous term that includes all forms of movement across institutions and countries as well as positions—from being a guest speaker or a one-year fellow–visiting scholar to sabbatical exchanges to more long-term movements. In the end, I decided to focus mainly on immigrants who made their mobility permanent by seeking (or already securing) a tenure-track position in a country other than the one where they were born and raised. In addition, while most of the research to date has focused on small cases in a specific national context, and mostly in Europe and Asia, I am focusing on an integrated analysis of movement from many countries to many countries with an emphasis on immigration to the United States.

I embarked originally on a "me-search" to understand my topic better but gradually became intrigued by broader questions: What prepares academics to make such a life-altering decision? Are there any childhood circumstances that can predict a predisposition? What motivates immigration? How well do academic immigrants integrate into their host institutions and cultures? What are the processes by which they feel "othered"? What challenges do they encounter in having their feet in two different worlds simultaneously? How do they maintain relationships with their home country? What do they miss? What value do they believe they bring to their institutions that stem from their foreignness? Do they expect to go back "home"? What is considered "home"?

These and many more questions constituted the basis for my in-depth personal interviews (with IRB authorization from Rutgers University) with eighty-one academics, in the fields with which I feel most comfortable—media, communication, journalism, advertising, and information—over about two years from 2019 to 2020.

I started by approaching immigrant colleagues and asked if they would be willing to be interviewed for this research project. Later I expanded my recruitment through a "snowball" method. This enabled me to extend invitations to colleagues of colleagues. The size of the pool of potential interviewees quickly became overwhelming. I was surprised at how collaborative and enthusiastic everyone approached was—whether they knew me or we had just met. They were highly motivated to share their experiences. As Jon (the United Kingdom to the United States) responded to my invitation, "Talking about myself for two hours? What's there not to like?" Of the eighty-three people I approached, only two turned me down (for reasons unrelated to the study). I stopped at eighty-one interviewees, as I felt I had reached a saturation point; that is, I felt that additional interviews, fascinating live histories as they were, would not likely add different insights or themes. In other words, these interviews would likely become too redundant.

The interview schedule was designed to tap into the following areas through the key questions below, adjusted with each interviewee as the interview unfolded:

1 Life history—Describe the general narrative of your childhood and education, family background, anything unusual, any international experiences, second language learning, and so forth.
2 Transition to another country—What were the circumstances that led to the transition, and why did you decide to stay once you were there?
3 Primary relationships—Re—parents/grandparents, children, spouse: how did they react to the move? Have they remained in the home country or moved with you/or somewhere else? How close are you to them now?
4 Identity—How do you define yourself? What do you miss about your home country (if at all), and what don't you miss

and prefer in your current situation? How well integrated do you feel? How involved with the host culture, politics, consumption of news, etc.?

Do you, and if so, how, maintain connections with your homeland—personal relationship, culture, current events, etc.? Do you continue to feel insider/outsider? When/if does it become particularly difficult for you? How do you handle it? Whom do you socialize with? Do you have a preference for co-patriots?

5. Academic work—How do you think the fact that you are an immigrant is affecting your academic work? Are there disadvantages to being an immigrant? Are you encountering language issues? Are there advantages to being an immigrant? Are there aspects in your work in which you feel different than your colleagues?

6. Demographics—Are there any specific issues related to your core demographic descriptors—your gender, race, or religion, as well as the intersectionality of your identities? Do you think there is a difference between being an academic immigrant and other kinds of immigrants?

7. Future—Are there identity issues related to raising your children in a host country, leaving aging parents in your home country, and thinking about your own trajectory toward retirement? Do you have any regrets? Do you have any desires or plans to return to your homeland? Have you been thinking about old age, death, and burial-related issues?

8. Others—I ended the interview with an open-ended question, about anything else they wished to share with me. This often opened a Pandora's box of stories.

As an interviewer, I often engage in reciprocal conversation, sharing my own experiences where appropriate. Doing so is sincere and has proven to be an effective strategy for creating trust and a dialogical interactional relationship. Two immigrants in conversation, sharing their experiences, and discovering commonalities and differences.

Throughout our time together, I made an effort to engage in authentic listening, which requires being mindfully present in the interaction, fully engaged in the listening and speaking as I was making an effort to build trustful relationships.[17] I very much liked to

Table 1.1
Participants' Demographics

	Gender M F	Race W B L AE AS ME	Seniority J S SR	Employment T TT O
N=81	33 48	41 5 9 10 12 4	11 57 13	65 4 12
%	41 59	51 6 11 12 15 5	14 70 16	80 5 15

Key:

Gender: M Male, F Female

Race/Ethnicity: W White, B Black, L Latino/a, AE Asian East, AS Asian South, ME Middle Eastern

Seniority in academia: J Junior (up to seven years beyond graduation), S Senior (eight years or more beyond graduation), SR (senior approaching retirement)

Employment status: T Tenured, TT Tenure Track, O Other—Non-tenure track, adjunct, temporary

borrow the concept of "participant listener" (parallel to that of "participant observer") from ethnography and from the Deep Listening movement in music.[18] This practice of radical attentiveness calls for the voluntary nature of listening over the involuntary nature of hearing. I also tried to really listen authentically and empathetically to my participants.

Many interviews were held in person during the annual meetings of the International Communication Association (ICA) and the Association of Education in Journalism and Mass Communication (AEJMC) in conference meeting rooms. Others took place in coffee shops, some during my visits to institutional offices, and several were completed online, especially the last few as we entered the early phase of COVID-19.

Of the eighty-one interviewees, forty-nine identified as females and thirty-two as males. They were diverse by age, race, ethnicity, religion, and country of origin, as well as by academic seniority, but they all earned a doctorate along the way. As Table 1.1 demonstrates, this was a privileged sample of academics: most of them were White, already seniors in academia, and tenured. While we do not have data for comparisons with this sample, and I am not making any claim for generalizability, I do submit that there is a lot we can learn from a group of academic immigrants who are well established and safely employed but remain a "migrant soul" (to borrow from the title of a book).[19]

This is also a good place to pause and distinguish these two terms—migrant and immigrant—and to explain my intentional choice to use the term "immigrant" to refer to my participants. The term "migrant" usually denotes a person in transit, moving from one place to another. Migrant workers, for example, in occupations such as agriculture, construction, and care work, are considered migrants. They follow employment opportunities, often sending their earnings back home to support their families, and are usually on temporary working visas. Illegal migrants, seeking to flee disaster or conflict areas and searching for a haven, are also best described as migrants, due to their movement, unstable residential status, and lack of permanency. Immigrants, on the other hand, are those who moved but established themselves in a new society. They integrate into their new home, often marry into it, raise children, and seek permanent residency. They mostly have no plans to return to their home country even though they maintain strong cultural, linguistic, and familial ties to it.

The vast majority of my study's participants (85 percent) fall within the definition of an immigrant, and only 15 percent could be considered still in transit. These migrants were at the time unsuccessful in securing a permanent academic position and were still seeking opportunities. In addition, a few of the well-established immigrants were adventurous and enjoyed the challenge of moving around to different cultures and academic settings but established themselves solidly in each of the new settings. A more appropriate term for these few is perhaps "academic nomads" or "academic wanderers" rather than "academic migrants." They choose to move from one place to another, enjoying the lack of permanency and wandering.

This is also a good place to reflect on another choice of terms: home country versus host country. Both are potentially contested terms: Home country refers to the country of origin, which may not feel like "home" anymore (and in some cases—never has). Host country refers to the destination country where the immigrant moved to, but that, too, is a limiting term: many of the immigrants do not feel they are "hosted," nor do they wish to be, as they want to feel at home in their new country. The term "new country" is also problematic, as it was for those immigrants in my study who have already lived there for decades; indeed, the term "new" reminds them that they have never been completely accepted. Given the complexities and the absence of a common alternative, I use all these terms interchangeably throughout the book to relate to the nexus of movement from the original country in which an interviewee grew up and the country in which he or she settled.

Collectively, my interviewees left thirty-seven countries around the world (Argentina, Australia, Barbados, Belgium, Brazil, Bulgaria, Cameroon, Canada, Chile, China, Colombia, Finland, France, Germany, Greece, Hong Kong, India, Iran, Ireland, Israel, Italy, Jordan, Kuwait, Mexico, New Zealand, Nigeria, Norway, Pakistan, Portugal, Puerto Rico, Romania, Russia, Rwanda, South Korea, Sweden, the United Kingdom, and the United States). They moved to eleven different countries (Belgium, Canada, Czech Republic, Israel, the Netherlands, New Zealand, Portugal, Singapore, Sweden, the United Kingdom, and the United States). The United States was by far the most common host country in my study—fifty-eight of my interviewees immigrated there (see Table 1.2).

Many of my interviewees were privileged, in many ways, moving from one high-resource industrialized country to another, even fitting well in terms of their embodied racial identity. They left their home country of their own accord; that is, they were not forced to move due to external forces. They were mostly tenured already or on a tenure track, and their legal residency status in their new country had been resolved. In this sense, their stories were less those of "precarity and resilience," which is the focus of the abovementioned edited collection of narratives of migrant academics from the global south to Europe.[20] Thus, we might say that their stories reveal to us what it means to be an academic immigrant in the best of situations.

To be clear, this book is not about institutions of higher education and their various manifestations and transitions around the world. Nor is it about neoliberal forces, erosion of academic freedom, labor struggles, gender and racial inequalities, ethnocentrism of teaching and scholarship, and the many other critiques of academia today. A lot has been written about these issues already, and while they provide the context in which my participants are embedded, these issues are well beyond the scope of this book. Furthermore, I also want to highlight in this book not only the challenges and structured inequalities in academia but also the value that academic immigrants bring to their institutions and their own empowered sense of self.

Interviews lasted for one to two hours. They were audio recorded and later transcribed verbatim. Interviewees received the transcripts and were allowed to edit and delete information that in retrospect they

Table 1.2
Study Participants

Name	From	To	Gender	Race	Seniority	Employment
Alisha	India	United States	F	AS	S	T
Amanda	United Kingdom	United States	F	W	SR	O
Anamika	India	United States	F	AS	S	T
Andres	Norway	United States	M	W	S	T
Anna	Cyprus/ Greece	United Kingdom	F	W	S	T
Anne	Canada	United Kingdom	F	W	S	T
Antonio	Puerto Rico	United States	M	L	SR	T
Armin	Barbados	United States	M	B	SR	T
Avi	Israel	United States	M	W	S	T
Charlotte	United States/ Israel	United Kingdom	F	W	S	T
Claire	Canada	United States	F	W	J	O
Constantinos	Greece	United States	M	W	S	O
Cosmas	Nigeria	United States	M	B	S	T
Cristina	Brazil	Portugal	F	L	S	O
Dana	Israel	United States	F	W	S	O
Daniela	Colombia	United States	F	L	S	T
Davide	Italy	United Kingdom	M	W	S	T
Demetrios	Greece	United States	M	W	S	T

Table 1.2 Continued
Study Participants

Name	From	To	Gender	Race	Seniority	Employment
Dick	United States / Europe	Singapore	M	W	SR	T
Doina	Romania	United States	F	W	S	O
Eddy	Europe	Israel	M	W	S	T
Edith	New Zealand	United Kingdom	F	W	S	T
Elena	Russia	United States	F	W	J	O
Emma	China	United States	F	AE	J	TT
Enrichetta	Italy	United States	F	W	S	T
Eva	Brazil	Sweden	F	L	S	T
Evan	Belgium	Europe	M	W	S	T
Fintan	Ireland	New Zealand Belgium	M	W	S	T
Florence	United States	Canada	F	W	S	T
Gaus	Pakistan	United States	M	ME	S	T
George	Romania	United States	M	W	S	T
Gisela	Germany	United States	F	W	S	T
Griet	Belgium	United States	F	W	S	T
Hadas	Israel	United States	F	W	S	T
Hassan	Iran	United States	M	ME	SR	T

(*Continued*)

Table 1.2 Continued
Study Participants

Name	From	To	Gender	Race	Seniority	Employment
HyeJin	South Korea	United States	F	AE	J	T
Ikechukwu	Nigeria	United States	M	B	S	T
Iracema	Brazil	Portugal	F	L	S	T
Jae-Joon	South Korea	United States	M	AE	S	T
Jennifer	United Kingdom	United States	F	W	SR	T
Jon	United Kingdom	United States	M	W	SR	T
Jose	Argentina	United States	M	L	S	T
Jozef	Belgium	United States	M	W	S	T
Juan	Mexico	United States	M	L	S	T
Juha	South Korea	United States	F	AE	S	T
Lara	United States	United Kingdom	F	W	S	T
Lars	United States	Singapore	M	W	SR	T
Lauren	United States	Canada	F	W	J	O
Leo Yin	China	United States	M	AE	S	T
Lillian	Canada	United States	F	W	S	T
Lior	Israel/ United States	Singapore	F	W	J	O
Lynn	United States	Europe	F	W	S	T
Maya	Israel	United Kingdom	F	W	S	T

Table 1.2 Continued
Study Participants

Name	From	To	Gender	Race	Seniority	Employment
Mayur	India	United States	M	AS	S	T
Meena	India	United States	F	AS	S	T
Mina	India	United States	F	AS	S	T
Mona	Kuwait	United States	F	ME	J	O
Nadya	Bulgaria	United States	F	W	S	T
Nathan	Israel	United States	M	W	J	O
Ning	China	United States	F	AE	S	T
Okeke	Rwanda	United States	M	B	S	T
Patrick	Scotland	Belgium	M	W	SR	T
Paula	Germany	United Kingdom	F	W	S	T
Rachel	Canada	United Kingdom	F	W	SR	T
Rhi Won	South Korea	United States	F	AE	J	TT
Richard	Australia	United States	M	W	SR	T
Rumia	India	United States	F	AS	S	T
Samina	India	United States	F	AS	S	T
Satya	India	Sweden	F	AS	S	O
Savitri	India	United States	F	AS	SR	T
Smita	India	United States	F	AS	S	T

(*Continued*)

Table 1.2 Continued
Study Participants

Name	From	To	Gender	Race	Seniority	Employment
Tamir	Israel	United States	M	W	S	T
Tanzoui	Cameroon	United States	M	B	S	T
Teresa	Puerto Rico	United States	F	L	S	T
Vihaan	India	United States	M	AS	S	T
Violeta	Chile	United States	F	L	SR	T
Wael	Jordan	United States	M	ME	J	TT
Xiao	China	United States	M	AS	S	T
Xiaolan	China	United States	F	AE	S	T
Yee	Hong Kong	United Kingdom	F	AE	S	T
Yerim	South Korea	United States	F	AE	J	TT

Key:

Gender: M Male, F Female

Race/Ethnicity: W White, B Black, L Latino/a, AE Asian East, AS Asian South, ME Middle Eastern

Seniority in academia: J Junior (up to seven years beyond graduation), S Senior (eight years or more beyond graduation), SR (senior approaching retirement)

Employment status: T Tenured, TT Tenure Track, O Other—Non–tenure track, adjunct, temporary

regretted sharing, as well as information they were concerned might reveal their identity. They were also allowed to propose a pseudonym for themselves that reflects their cultural background. This was particularly important to guarantee that interviewees' anonymity was protected and to facilitate intimate and sincere conversations on many sensitive issues. In cases where an interviewee's identity might be easily revealed through a unique story, I refrained from naming the individual country and used a regional term such as "Europe." I also replaced the names of specific locations and institutions with more general regional terms and only used pseudonyms to protect the identity of my participants.

Throughout the book, I provide many detailed verbatim quotes (with very minor and rare edits for English clarity). In cases of edits, I used the sign [. . .] to indicate that text has been removed (either for being redundant, irrelevant to the point I am making, or unclear). In contrast, the use of three periods . . . indicates a pause in the interviewee's flow of words. I also include occasional editorial comments in [], such as replacing names or offering an explanation for a concept or name used.

Many of the participants shared with me that the interview was a very meaningful form of self-reflection. Three of my interviewees who moved from India to the United States expressed it very colorfully. Mayur wrote in an email to me following the interview, "I want to thank you for giving me this opportunity of self-discovery. It allowed me to not only open up on these issues but also encounter some self-exploration questions that I hadn't before in this way." Other expressions included "It has a healing effect on me" (Mina); "It made me think about so many things. Things that lurk under the surface but seldom come to the fore" (Rumia).

In terms of analyses, the life-history transcripts were analyzed by keywords and themes, using NVivo software, as well as by reading and re-reading the interviews, as is the customary practice in qualitative methods of analysis. I was aided by the framework offered by the "flexible coding" approach that recognizes that analysis is initiated by the built-in interview protocol, and thus is not entirely inductive.[21] The questions I posed to my interviewees structured the conversations and thus led to the broad themes presented in this book. However, given the nature of the heterogeneous, highly intelligent, and informed nature of the participants in the study, our conversations meandered away from my questions in completely unexpected directions, creating a vast list of codes that were investigated with the help of the NVivo software.

The Book

My initial analysis led me to publish selected findings in an article and an opinion commentary (see below) that focused on selected aspects of the immigration experience. The feedback I received from readers, some participants in the study with whom I shared the publications, and other readers new to me, was heartwarming. Correspondents cited that they found themselves in the pages, claiming that I was expressing their own experiences and that it felt empowering and healing to them. For example, Yufeng, a junior male faculty member originally from China, wrote to me (from an email received on February 5, 2024),

> I took a close look at both pieces this weekend, and they both deeply resonated with my personal experiences and my ongoing reflections on my ever-shifting positionality in research and teaching—they all felt deeply personal and emotional! I greatly appreciate the time and effort you took to undertake this important work, seeking to elevate the shared voices and experiences of often othered immigrant researchers like us. It prompted me to reflect again on my own experiences, and I've noted some of my thoughts below. They're quite lengthy.

I felt great joy with this rewarding feedback, and it motivated me to proceed with this more ambitious project: of sharing more broadly what I found from my interviewees.

What I hope to accomplish in this book is to elevate our colleagues' voices, not through theorizing them or embedding them in the vast existing literature on immigration, identity politics, or higher education. Instead, I wish for their voices to be heard as if they are part of an informal conversation, in our department's coffee corner, the institution's cafeteria, the corridor, or a conference room. Doing so will let you get to know them better and appreciate them as colleagues through the retelling of their narratives within the analytical structure that I was able to create. In particular, I am writing this book with special care to make it accessible, grounded, and relatable. I am limiting the use of scholarly citations (and leaving them as endnotes, so they can be ignored if one pleases to do so) and trying to avoid jargonistic academic language that excludes so many readers.

This book is divided into nine chapters, including this one. Chapter 2, "The Seeds," lays out childhood stories about circumstances and experiences that may have predisposed the participants to immigrate for academic life at a later stage of life. Interviewees discussed cultural experiences, travel, second language learning, and media exposure during childhood—among others—that opened them to the world outside their original ones and pulled them to move and explore other places.

Chapter 3, "The Voyage," discusses the motivations and circumstances that led to the move from their home country to a new one and focuses on the 3Ps outlined above: the personal, professional, and political reasons for uprooting and migrating.

Chapter 4, "The Challenges," goes deeper into narratives of challenges encountered through the first stage of the transition as well as those that remain ongoing both in the culture-at-large in which they reside and in academia more specifically. Those vary from adjusting to the weather, learning cultural norms of discourse and behavior, language challenges, being "othered," and even being discriminated against.

Chapter 5, "The Benefits," counterbalances the struggles with the challenges with a strong sense of value that the academic immigrants bring to their institutions of higher education in the three pillars of academic life: scholarship, teaching, and service. They are proud of their unique positions as insiders-outsiders that allow them to offer unique contributions to academia.

Chapter 6, "The Home," discusses specific issues of belonging and identity as well as the sense of living double lives. On a continuum between full integration to complete alienation, most of the interviewees find themselves somewhere in the middle, never really integrated completely but enough to be at peace with the life they established.

Chapter 7, "The Bridge," describes the various ways academic immigrants bridge their double life experiences: whether bonding with compatriots and maintaining cultural and culinary traditions at home, using various forms of digital media to keep in touch with current events and culture, and regular visits to the home country when possible.

Chapter 8, "The Return," explores motivations and fantasies about going back to the homeland, reflections over aging, death, and burial, and the realization of most that they will never actually go back and that "back" does not exist anymore.

Finally, Chapter 9, "The Support," pulls the strings of the main themes of the book together and proposes suggestions for possible action steps that institutions of higher education can take to foster a culture of belonging and maximize the benefits that academic immigrants can bring to them, individually, as well as to students, colleagues, their discipline, and your institution's community. Advancing such suggestions in an era where immigration is so prevalent may enable academia to serve as a role model for other social institutions as well. The book concludes with a postscript, where I share some reflections about the current phase of my journey.

Thanks

I have integrated into this book content from earlier articles based on this study, with copyright permission, which I am thankful for:

> A research article: Lemish, D. (2022). "Home no home: Academic immigrants in the fields of communication," *International Journal of Communication* 16, Feature 4424–4436. https://ijoc.org/index.php/ijoc/article/viewFile/19994/3891
>
> A commentary: Lemish, D. (2022). "Academic immigrants in DEI discussions: Another blind spot. *Change: The Magazine of Higher Learning*, 54(3), 51–55. 10.1080/00091383.2022.2054200
>
> An advice column is integrated into chapter 9, with gratitude for the copyright permission: Lemish, D. (August 21, 2023). Ten ways to support your immigrant colleagues. *Academic Leader*. https://www.academic-leader.com/topics/institutional-culture/ten-ways-to-support-your-immigrant-colleagues/

My special thanks are extended to the members of the School of Communication and Information at Rutgers University for the nourishing environment it provided me, and to Dr. Diana Floegel, who at the time in her role as an outstanding research assistant transcribed the interviews and conducted the first round of coding of themes in NVivo. Dr. Peter Lemish, my lifelong partner and development editor, and a twice-academic immigrant himself (the United States to Israel and Israel to the United States), has been instrumental throughout this project and the ideas within, as always.

And finally, and most importantly, I am deeply grateful to my eighty-one participants in the study who let me into their private and professional lives, and the many more who shared their stories with me when hearing about this project. I hope you will continue to find yourselves between the lines.

2

The Seeds

Do Childhood Experiences
Prepare for Immigration?

"I Knew There Was More Out There in the World"

My study revealed that the academic immigrants I interviewed do not seem to have chosen immigration randomly. Many among them had some kind of childhood background or experiences that opened them to cultures and languages other than their own that expanded their horizons and curiosity to worlds beyond the one in which they grew up. I have no pretensions here to offer psychological analyses into my interviewees' souls, as I do not have the appropriate training or permission to do so; nor were the interviews intended to be therapeutic in nature. The observations I am offering here are only based on the participants' own retelling and self-reflections.

This noted, I must admit that the interviewees' predispositions strongly resonated with my own childhood experience. I spent two years at the end of the 1950s in New York City from the age of five to seven with my parents and my older sister, when my father was on an educational mission. Transferring from Israel at a period of postindependence nation-building and austerity and landing in the hustle and bustle of New York City with what seemed at the time as an overwhelming abundance was a life-changing experience. I was introduced to television for the first time, to skyscrapers, department store displays, and Broadway musicals. I went to a toy store where I picked out my very own crying-peeing doll for my birthday (I still have it on the shelf in my home office). I went to an English-speaking school and swore allegiance to the American flag every morning. I encountered a Christmas tree and Santa Claus for the first time, and so discovered that I am Jewish and different (I had no idea beforehand, as everyone was Jewish where I grew up). We traveled as a family from coast to coast, experiencing many of the most famous national parks and iconic sites in the United States. Those two years were burned in my consciousness forever as special, attractive, and full of unrestricted promise.

Upon our return to Israel, our home was forever visited by American colleagues, friends, and extended family relatives thereafter, and it was no surprise that learning the English language in school came easily to me later. My father continued to travel a lot over the years, to bring with him upon return stories, little souvenirs, and photos and slides he has taken from around the world, and we all have been "infected" by the traveling desire—"virus," as we called it at home. Put me on a plane and I will go anywhere, anytime, I used to say. Just to experience new places, new cultures, new people, new smells and tastes, new possibilities. For years I would accept any invitation to give a keynote or a presentation or participate in a workshop anywhere in the world, whether convenient or not. I traveled to Australia twice (thirty-six hours each way) for a two-day conference. No effort, jet lag, or preparation for a research presentation would keep me from reliving the awe that travel inspired in me, since my childhood experiences.

My family background and childhood experiences could also explain why continuing to higher education was taken for granted and never challenged. My father was an economist with a master's degree and my mother completed a teacher preparation seminar after her high school studies. My sister earned a master's in clinical psychology, and our youngest brother completed his degree in labor studies. Education was highly valued at our home and assumed as a natural progression of life: you attend preschool and kindergarten, complete elementary school, then high school, then you do your mandatory military service, and then you go to the university. On the way, you are also probably going to get married and start a family. Unsurprisingly perhaps, given my thirst for travel, I chose to study geography for my undergraduate studies, concentrating on human and social geography (rather than physical geography such as geomorphology and geology). Also, quite predictable, as some family members would say years later, I ended up marrying a social justice activist man and engaged scholar from California (rather than a "salt of the earth" Israeli), going with him to graduate school in the United States, having three dual-citizen children, and many years later, ending in the United States, where I am writing these lines now.

In reflecting on my life trajectory, I believe that my U.S. childhood experience probably prepared the ground and fertilized a lot of what was to come later in life for me, just like for many of the participants in my study. With similar experiences shared by many of the interviewees as they reflected on their childhood, they seemed to have accepted immigration as a sensible life change. In retelling their childhood narratives, several themes emerged quite regularly: family compositions, backgrounds, and contexts; the importance of education; early travel and foreign language experiences; and the role of media.

Family Background

Many of the interviewees assigned significant importance to their family background as an explanatory force for their life trajectory. Just growing up in cosmopolitan environments was proposed as cultivating a predisposition to immigration, as shared by Rumia (India to the United States):

> I think where I was born and the way I grew up had a pretty strong impact on how I view who I am in the world, and my relationship to difference and exploring or wanting to be—or my interest and curiosity in people from different cultures. I was born and grew up in New Delhi, and because it's a capital city, and given the kinds of schools I went to, I was exposed growing up to people from many different places. Not just from the West, but also from other parts like Japan, China, and Russia . . . so for me, I was always interested in the world. And I think that did shape what happened to me later in life.

Similarly, Juha (South Korea to the United States) related a unique family background that cultivated a clear path for herself:

> Since I was young, I always thought—that's what I'm going to do when I graduate from college [continue for a Ph.D.]. I think my dad influenced me. I was born in Seoul. But then we moved to a city that's kind of a Silicon Valley, where all the science-related institutions and technology companies are located. So, the town had so many Ph.Ds. A mom and dad—often, like, especially dads, they are the Ph.Ds. They have Ph.Ds from other countries; mostly the United States or the United Kingdom. So, I was just surrounded by this academic environment. And both of my uncles are professors in South Korea. They both got their degrees from the United States. So it was very natural to me. I wasn't thinking much. Honestly.

Antonio (Puerto Rico to the United States) was raised for a few years in New York City by his independent divorced mother before returning to Puerto Rico. While living in poverty, he recalls a stimulating childhood:

> For all the hardships that my mom went through, we were living right next to the university in [name of city], where her older brother was a professor of botany. So that environment, with all of the challenges—and there were many, financially especially for my mother—was very stimulating intellectually, as the university was my backyard. My playground. And I even got to help my uncle take care of his greenhouse for a while and go on field trips and see his slideshows as he traveled the world and came back to tell the family about his travels.

But not all childhood experiences were smooth and happy ones. Some were complicated and painful. Lara (United States to the United Kingdom), for example, described her difficult childhood circumstances and added, "In any case, the reason why I'm saying this is that this is a very formative story for me. Like, it was very formative to grow up on welfare for me. And all sorts of my perspective on life, like becoming, you know, a left academic, I mean, all of this stuff."

Childhood poverty was a shared experience for several other interviewees and impacted their views of the world. Satya (India to Sweden), for example, grew up in a refugee environment:

> I grew up in a neighborhood where everybody had almost the same history. They were all refugees, they were related to Pakistan, so we grew up with those stories. The interesting thing is that we never heard a word against Islam. Not once. The only thing that we heard about was that they had so much wealth that they left behind because they had to rush to leave the country. They had gold that they put in pots and they dug it underground, that someday they'll get back and get it. And they started from scratch.

The sense of temporality, of aspiring to "go back" is something that kept creeping into Satya's own immigration story, with its concerns about impermanence, as was unveiled later in the conversation.

A difficult childhood narrative of a mixed marriage and nationality was related by Anna (Cyprus/Greece to the United Kingdom):

> My dad is from Cyprus and my mom is from Greece. So, I was born in Cyprus, in Nicosia, the capital city. At a very young age, the age of three, I experienced war and the divide of Cyprus. I have very vivid memories in the way that a young child has very vivid memories of first the coup and the tanks that were in front of our house. I remember us fleeing so that my dad would not be summoned by the coup government to work on the national broadcaster. I remember the Turkish planes flying over our heads and so on. [. . .] One thing that is worth perhaps mentioning about my childhood, which I think is also determining both my experience with migration and also being someone who studies migration and ethnicity, is that I always remember my mom—even though she lived fifty years in Cyprus, she made a family there, her children were born in Cyprus—she would always consider herself a migrant. For her, it was always like, "I'm a foreigner here. I'm a migrant."

As Anna's immigration narrative unfolded later in the interview, it became clear how her family's background predisposed her to uproot, move around, and continue to have mixed affinities and a migrant sensibility. She added, "And also the other thing that of course shaped me is that I grew up in a country which is tiny but has been divided. And I was always very aware of the politics of ethnicity and the politics of division. And being very critical as a result of the politics of nationalists that create wars and divide countries and so on."

The Importance of Education

Whether parents were highly or poorly educated, well-to-do or poor, many of them prioritized their children's education and conveyed its importance to them. Jozef (Belgium to the United States) explained, "My grandfather was the youngest son of a local primary school teacher. And I think he was kind of the driving force behind the family. So, I think education was a big deal for him."

Similarly, Constantinos (Greece to the United States) said,

> In Greek society, there was this idea that everybody had to go to college. Everybody has to be educated. You need to equip the kids with as much knowledge as possible so they can succeed. So, if you don't go to college, you're not technically considered successful. Which is a very big, I think, difference, compared to here. So that's where that came from.

Different versions of the same motivation repeated itself in different cultures and social classes, as Richard (Australia to the United States) recalled this about his family's background: "My parents, simple farmers as they were, recognized the value of education. And that was given priority to all of our family members. My two eldest sisters went off to become nurses. Another sister became a primary school teacher. [. . .] We knew that life on the farm was not our destiny."

Similarly, Avi (Israel to the United States), too, described his parents' devotion to education:

> They were never formally educated because they were on the run. However, they had an appreciation for education. And so it was a lot of push from home for all of us to excel, and my dad was a merchant marine seaman. He would go for extended long periods as part of work, for a few months at a time. And being the eldest meant that I also took responsibility for the education of my siblings. So, when we had, you

know, the parent-teacher conferences, my mom would typically go to my teacher and I would go to my siblings' teachers, who used to be my teachers too. So there was kind of always emphasis on education, always got books for holidays and birthdays and so forth.

The same emphasis on education was recalled by Lynn (the United States to Europe), coming from a completely different cultural-religious background than Jewish Avi above:

I grew up in, like, the real poverty that people talk about and probably don't really know in experience. The church helped us get scholarships to go to Catholic grade school because the school system was not safe, and my parents really wanted us to get a good education. So, as long as we could, we were in grade school in Catholic school, all of us. My aunts and uncles helped pay. We had private donations from neighbors and staff that helped us go to school. I got a job when I was eleven. You weren't allowed to have working papers until you were thirteen, so I worked under the table so I could help and pay for my education.... I remember I saved for, like, seven months for a pair of sneakers so I could go to gym class with shoes that didn't have holes in them."

Parental devotion and sacrifice for their children's education was a theme that cut across many narratives from different cultures. Mina (India to the United States) said,

There was a lot of emphasis on a well-rounded education growing up. My parents basically sacrificed a lot to make sure that we were both very well educated. And so, I remember my mom actually not letting me do any housework or anything, which is odd, you know. But she was so particular that I should be independent when I grew up, and financially independent, not be a housewife, that she would say, "I'll take care of everything, you just study. You just do well." And, like, we would go all the way across the city to find a good tutor for my music. And all of that.

Anna (Cyprus/Greece to the United Kingdom) recalled a similar family priority: "So, my parents were always—even though they spent times in their life when they had very little time, very little money, it was always clear that if one thing is worth paying for, it's education. So, in that way, you know, basically, my father got a loan so I could go and do my master's in the U.S."

A few of my interviewees came from academic families where parents served as role models and pursuing higher education was perceived as a given expectation. Mayur (India to the United States) shared such a background: "Because of my dad who had done all those degrees and had a Ph.D. and was a professor, almost from the beginning it was my path. Like, it was a role model that I was also going to keep going for higher education and kind of be a professor, you know." And Elena (Russia to the United States), whose both parents went to university, said, "Yeah, so, I finished high school and then, well, since—both my parents, they were in the university. So, for them, it was kind of a logical thing for me, that I would do that as well. [...] Maybe their parents got some education beyond high school, but it was not, like, this kind of academic scholarly education. So, for my parents, it was important, and they certainly encouraged me to go to St. Petersburg State University, where they went."

Thus, a family background that is open to heterogeneous cultural experiences and values and invests in the education of their offspring seems to offer a fertile ground not only for completing higher education degrees but also for exploring possibilities outside of one's home country.

Travel and Languages

Some of the participants moved a lot during childhood, and they believed this prepared them to pick up and move later in life. For example, Amanda (the United Kingdom to the United States) shared,

> Well, I guess one unusual thing about me relevant to your project is that I moved a lot as a child. My father [...] often got posted to various places around the U.K. So I went to about twelve different schools. So, I think, that's what made me interested in communication, in a way. Because across the U.K there are very different ways of communicating. Different accents, different traditions, and so in a way, that was kind of an interesting upbringing. And one that, I suppose, made me less daunted by the idea that we'd just jump up and move ...

Similarly, Maya (Israel to the United Kingdom) related,

> My father worked for the Ministry of Foreign Affairs, so when I was five years old, we were relocated first to Istanbul for two years and then moved again to Brussels for two years, and then we returned to Israel but moved from the north to the center of the country. I had a lot of moving. I was a nomad. [...] I think that when I moved to London, it was obviously a very big move and it was a very momentous thing in my life. But I think there was something about me having been almost "trained" to land on my feet. Try to learn the cultural codes, quite quickly, as well as the language, because I spoke fluently Turkish when we were in Istanbul, and then I spoke fluently French.

A unique experience was shared by Anamika (India to the United States), who described herself as a "third culture kid," referring to children who are raised in a culture other than their parents' or their original nationality, and also spent a significant period during their childhood in yet another environment, thus experiencing a variety of cultural influences.[1] "I was a third culture kid, which means that I didn't belong to any one culture, and we were kind of separated from the local population." Anamika attended an American school in the Philippines and described her multicultural and linguistic experience: "So, growing up, I was learning a little smattering of Tagalog [a variant of Filipino] in the streets, and learned Punjabi and Hindi growing up, and then English starting when I was three already in India, and then opted for Spanish in the American school in the Philippines."

The frequent experience of relocation of "third culture kids" seems to prepare them to be able to adjust more easily to new cultural environments and to be open to learning new languages while at the same time not necessarily becoming overly tied to one or the other.[2] As a result, they may be searching for a clear sense of "home" that lingers into their adulthood, an issue we will return to in chapter 6. The spontaneous reference by Anamika to herself as a third culture kid is an instance that demonstrates the self-reflective nature of many of the interviews and the ability of these scholars to integrate their disciplinary expertise in thinking about their own experiences, as many of the quotes in this book suggest.

While Teresa (Puerto Rico to the United States) did not use the term "third culture kid," she had a somewhat similar experience of moving around and experiencing cultures differing from her parents' backgrounds and her nationality. "We would come and go. I was born in Germany, and when I was six months old, we came back. And then we stayed in the United States, and then we came back to Germany. So, in the meantime, my dad went to Vietnam. So that year, my family went to Puerto Rico while my dad went to Vietnam." The need to move around and the ability to settle and thrive in different cultures as a dominant part of childhood's lived experience was shared by quite a few of the participants in the study.

Having parents of mixed-cultural backgrounds opened the horizons for several of my interviewees. Growing up in Greece, Demetrios (Greece to the United States), for example, whose mother is American, did a lot of traveling: "We did travel, growing up, a fair amount between the U.S. and Greece. My mother's family was all here [in the United States], and we were fairly close. We were very close to my grandparents, and so we could come, every year or every two years to the U.S. for either Christmas or summertime vacation."

Parental engagement in political and cultural turmoil impacted a few of my participants, including Jon (the United Kingdom to the United States). His left-leaning activist parents brought him along as they traveled a lot during his childhood when they were engaged in political resistance: "So, my parents took me to Yugoslavia which they went to because it was not aligned with Russia's communist country. And they took me then, I think we went to Norway the following year. And then we went to Yugoslavia three times the following years before I grew out of it." Travel motivated by politics, activism, and social difference was thus not a new experience for him.

Other interviewees traveled the world for vacations and family visits during their childhood, acquired foreign languages, or had international visitors hosted in their homes. Lauren (the United States to Canada), for example, shared stories of family vacations growing up:

> England, Europe, learning different languages ... it's all—I mean, it's why I was eager to leave [a Midwest U.S. city].... Because I knew there was more out there in the world. I think that when you're not exposed at a young age, you don't necessarily know that. So I was super eager. I was ready to pick up and move. That's the truth of it."

And Eva (Brazil to Sweden) related similar curiosity for different experiences: "We traveled most inside the country. But I think it was very much like a cultural thing, knowing different places, different cultures."

From the other side of the globe, Edith (New Zealand to the United Kingdom) described,

> My family traveled a lot when I was young. We did a lot of trips as a family. But we also lived, when I was, I think, the ages of about seven to ten, we lived in Canada for three and a half years. My father is a scientist. And he got a job—I believe it was working for the Canadian government in some way. He's always worked for governments. So, he took us to Canada. We lived in Ottawa for three and a half years. And it was very formative; I remember it very well. We had a great time. [. . .] So, growing up, I had quite a lot of experience of travel to other parts of the world."

In response to my question about childhood experiences, Evan (Belgium to Europe) explained,

> My parents' generation was the first to start traveling. So, the traditional old-school Belgian way of holidays was going to the Belgian coast. In particular, to a coastal resort where the entire city of Antwerp went to in summer. But when I was around twelve, then my parents started taking me on longer travels in Europe. And they had some strange affinity with the Channel Islands. So, for some weird reason, I ended up there quite often.

It was revealing to find out that similar experiences were shared by participants growing up in very different cultures, national contexts, and circumstances. Wael (Jordan to the United States), for example, who comes from a very different background, emphasized the role of foreign languages in his upbringing: "My mother started teaching us English from an early age before we started at school. My mother is also a reader. Like, even outside of just strictly for educational purposes. So, we started reading at an early age, you know, books in Arabic, English, and French. There was a lot of focus on academics generally, I think." Language education and travel were tied together in his life narrative as well: "We traveled in the area in general. We went to Egypt, and Syria, back in the time when you could actually travel to Syria. Lebanon. We have some relatives in Lebanon as well. It's the Middle East, you know, so in each of them there's always a new ancient culture to see somewhere. Not that Jordan is lacking, though."

Evan, whose life took him to various European locations, continued to explain his openness to learning many languages, a key feature for cultural adjustment: "Language is more complicated because you shouldn't forget the Belgian context here. There are three official languages: Dutch—some would call it Flemish, but I prefer Dutch—French, and German. And of course, English was and still is omnipresent. So, I got the confrontation with the foreign languages at a very early age."

Whether from Oceania, Latin America, or the Middle East, academics who experienced exposure to difference via travel and second (and third) language learning during their earlier years seemed to have a greater openness to moving around as adult academics.

The Role of Media

The availability of traditional media, including books and magazines, was often tied into the narratives and had a memorable place in the stories shared by my interviewees. For example, Lars (the United States to Singapore) reminisced, "One of my earlier memories in this context is that my dad had an issue of *National Geographic* called *The British Way*. It was a history of the British Empire. And three, four nights a week we would go through the same issue and we would talk about the history and culture of England."

Antonio (Puerto Rico to the United States) recalled, "In my years as a middle school and high school student, I delivered an English-language newspaper in my hometown. And in that hour of walking and delivering the newspaper door to door, I read it from front to cover. Usually, the sports section was to the front, but I was aware of what was going on in the world. So that helped me keep a view of the world that was a bit different."

And Meena (India to the United States) shared these memories: "From an early age I heard stories of Europe and grew up with all the knick-knacks they [parents] brought back as well as albums full of photos of their travels through western Europe. [...] So, I guess there was that sort of allure, and they had all their pictures of traveling all over Europe and seeing the Eiffel Tower and all of that. So, it was an opening to, I suppose, an international world. Through their stories, through their photographs."

For Xiao (China to the United States), it was the old-fashioned radio that opened his eyes to the world: "I was in a school that places a lot of emphasis on the study of foreign languages [...] and we were encouraged to listen to short-wave radio, to the BBC and the VOA [Voice of America]. ... So everybody had a short-wave radio and we listened to these international radio broadcasts."

Also from China, the junior male faculty member whom I mentioned in chapter 1 wrote to me with his response, "My curiosity about the world was largely shaped by television shows and media. I vividly remember being inspired by watching the American TV show *The Amazing Race* as a child. This spurred me to travel around the world on my own during and after my undergraduate years in Singapore, including visits to often othered countries/places like Nepal, Tibet, North Korea, Iran, Cuba, among others. These experiences eventually led me to the United States to pursue my MSW and later my Ph.D. [from an email received on February 5, 2024]."

As might be expected, reading played an important role during childhood in opening the world to the interviewees. Cristina (Brazil to Portugal) shared that her mother passed away when she was a child and she went through a very unhappy childhood with her father and her older brothers:

> I had to learn how to deal with my own things. All these things that most children and/or girls go through with their mother's support, I didn't have that. So, I had to grow up quite quickly. And also, I was quite focused on school. And since I was the youngest one in my house, and also the only girl, I was quite introverted. I spent a great deal of time reading. I would say that's what created all my desires, wishes, and dreams. Because since I was very young, very little, I had this dream or goal of leaving Brazil. And when I look back, especially to my childhood, I believe that was related to that. I spent a great deal of time when I was a child reading.

While Juan's (Mexico to the United States) family background was quite different, he, too, assigned great importance to the books he was exposed to during childhood:

> And there was something about the way that my parents brought normal behaviors that were not necessarily about learning traditional ways, but they brought books to the house. And for people who didn't have much education, they had that—they subscribed to that Reader's Digest system where they would get one new great work of literature per month. And they subscribed to encyclopedias also that you got in installments. So, you would get literally one encyclopedia letter per month or week or whatnot. But I remember by the time I was maybe eight, nine, ten, I had access to a collection of 200 masterpieces in literature, and more than one encyclopedia in my house, which was extremely rare in my circle. My friends wouldn't have that in their homes.

In summary, these varying childhood experiences may offer a perspective to academics' openness to seek change, uproot, explore differences, and adjust. Early multicultural and multilanguage experiences through travel, living circumstances, familial compositions, and media exposure were often associated in the participants' own narratives with their adult immigration story. The emphasis their families put on education served as a driving force to pursue higher education and academic careers. These backgrounds may also be at the heart of many academic immigrants' scholarly curiosity and inner drive, as we will explore later on.

3
The Voyage

What Are the Reasons for Immigration?

"I Think We've Accidentally Immigrated"

With similar childhood and coming-of-age experiences shared by many of the interviewees, they seemed to have accepted immigration as a sensible life change. As I reflected earlier upon my own journey, most made their decision out of choice for a variety of personal, professional, and political reasons (which I coined the "3Ps"), oftentimes for a mixture of the three. All three groups of reasons operated as both push and pull reasons: pushing away from their home country and pulling over to a new one.

Personal Reasons

There are multitudes of personal reasons that lead individuals to leave their birth country and move somewhere else. Some of the most prevalent ones surfaced in the recounting by the interviewees. These included following a partner, as was the case for Avi (Israel to the United States), who met his American wife during graduate school and shared his internal deliberations: "You know, the whole notion of raising a family, and the fact that the transition [to Israel] would probably be more difficult on her than it would be on me [to stay in the United States]." Nadya (Bulgaria to the United States) related, "The initial plan was, with the boyfriend I had, we were going to wrap up here and then go back to Europe, not necessarily back to Bulgaria, but back to Europe somewhere. [...] But then over time, during my Ph.D. program, after I broke up with my early Bulgarian boyfriend, I met someone else in my doctoral program, an American partner, who is not very moveable. He doesn't necessarily want to go live in Europe. So yeah, we have now been together for the past ten years or so. At this point, you know, now I already kind of have a life here." Dick (the United States to multiple locations) shared: "I started my Ph.D. in the U.S. and met a woman from Norway and went to Norway, and back and forth. But then I met another woman in Norway who became my wife, and the rest is history. So staying is staying. [...] It was like 'Maybe I'll be there, maybe not.' One thing led to another."

A few of the interviewees who married a member of the host society decided to stay for the sake of the children born in that relationship, including situations of complicated divorces. One such example came from a European interviewee: "I think I stayed because of the children. Because getting back home and getting the children back with me would have meant a horrible legal fight. Since I accepted early, it was logical to stay. Maybe I wasn't strong enough; maybe I didn't fight. [...] So I stayed because I thought, 'I'm not going to take the children away from their mother.'" Other sacrifices were made to keep a relationship intact, like Enrichetta (Italy to the United States), who followed her boyfriend and shared her story: "So I applied for a fellowship at my university to study abroad [to follow her boyfriend]. I otherwise would have never wanted to come to the U.S. The U.S. never excited me as a place where, you know, you would like to live your life. Well, I would think, France always intrigued me. Maybe Spain. But honestly, the U.S.—never. Ideologically, because you know, growing up quite leftist, the U.S. was the evil of unbridled capitalism and individualism and everything that is wrong with that. So, I guess that is why I always kept a distance between me and this country. Always."

Other personal reasons were mainly related by women and included looking for a fresh start after a painful divorce (a U.S. woman moving to Europe); getting away from a toxic relationship (a woman from Colombia to the United States) and from oppressive family dynamics (a woman from India moving to the United States). Elena (Russia to the United States) shared, "I really had, like, a bad year when my dog died, my boyfriend dumped me, and I was like, 'Okay, maybe I just need to change everything.' And at that point, I was talking to that guy from Iran. And I was like, 'Maybe, maybe that's what I can do.' And then I started really seriously investigating. And basically, like, a year after that I spent preparing and applying. And then the next year I came to the U.S."

Daniela (Colombia to the United States) shared a complicated personal story that required outside assistance to resolve:

> The dean kind of took us [Daniela and her husband] under his wing. And we actually partied with him and he took us to dinners and, you know, things like that. And then, he knew that the relationship was going through very, very rocky times. We were, like, really in bad shape. Both of us. So, one day, I made an appointment with the dean, and I went to his office and said, "You've seen us. This is not going anywhere. I think the only way to cut this off is for me to leave the country. 'Cause someone has to leave. As long as we are in the same city and the same country, we're gonna run into each other. We're gonna, you know, keep spiraling down. He's not going to go anywhere. I speak English and French. I'll go. And I have my parents in the U.S. Help me find a scholarship." And he did.

Often one thing led to another, and a temporary arrangement became permanent. Such was the case for Anne and her husband, who immigrated from Canada to the United Kingdom: "We were thinking, 'This is probably maybe a five-year thing, and then we go back [...] but you know, we both started progressing in our career [...] and then, one day, we just kind of thought, you know, our son was well into primary school and all of that and we thought 'I think we've accidentally immigrated.'"

Sometimes it was following in the footsteps of siblings that facilitated the immigration. Yee (Hong Kong to the United Kingdom) related:

> Well, I decided to come to England. Because my two brothers both studied in England... and I just wanted to be away. You know, see the world kind of thing. So, I came as well. And even though I could

have stayed in Hong Kong to study, I had some sense that if I liked it, I would like to stay. But it wasn't, like, a plan of, you know, education and immigration kind of plan. But I always thought that I would do my A-levels [examinations] and then, you know, I would like to carry on studying in the U.K. Again because, you know, both my brothers did, and so, yeah, that was what went through my mind.

In other cases, it was a cultural expectation, a "rite of passage," as Edith suggests (New Zealand to the United Kingdom):

My dad was an immigrant himself, and my mom is a few generations back in New Zealand. [. . .] I went to university here in New Zealand. But there's a real tradition, at a certain point, of doing what's called your OE, your overseas experience. Because New Zealand is so far away from everywhere else in the world. You know, it's almost like a real rite of passage. You leave, then you go away. And often, especially, you go somewhere like London or Europe where you have a kind of family roots, if you are white, right? White, as they call it, Pākehā, New Zealander, you often have roots back to some part of the U.K. and Europe. You go back to explore those. [. . .] Here was a kind of a real tradition of travel and seeing the world, I suppose, as I grew up. And we were privileged and lucky enough to do so.

Whatever the circumstances, fulfilling personal needs, whether socialized by society or born out of concrete need, played an important role in motivating people to first, move, and then—stay in the new place.

Professional Reasons

Professional reasons were often entangled with personal ones, being offered attractive jobs upon completion of the Ph.D. or the prospects of higher salaries and quality of life. These were particularly dominant in the stories of immigrants from Asia to the United States, where such moves were perceived as desirable by family members and society at large, and accepted with great pride. The concept of the "American Dream" was very much alive in their stories. This was less the case in countries with very strong national identities, such as Israel, where a move away was also stained with a sense of betrayal of the homeland, or

Canada, where members brought with them a cynical view of the inferiority of the United States' political system and dominant ideologies. Armin (Barbados to the United States) explained the circumstances pushing people out of Barbados and added, "I realized that to pursue an academic future, it would be less likely to be in the Caribbean than in the U.S. The opportunity to do things, the areas of research that I was invested in, all of that meant to me an immigration possibility." Xiao (China to the United States) related his familiarity with university life in China, saying, "That's something I really feel uncomfortable with. Those promotion procedures and so on. [. . .] The criteria are not clearly spelled out. And sometimes not at all fair." Additional perspective from China was offered by Ning (China to the United States): "At the time, economic reasons. The salary is very competitive now, but before I came here, I earned a salary of probably not even 100 U.S. dollars, as a university professor." In some cultural contexts, there were very limited academic opportunities altogether. Such, for example, was the advice that Gaus (Pakistan to the United States) received: "And then a friend went there, and he was like 'Okay, so, when you go back with a Ph.D., no one is going to value that. So, because you will not a find a good career.' Even if you have a Ph.D. [there are] the loopholes in the system back home."

Weighing the possible career trajectory if one is to stay in the home country versus moving away was also shared by Daniela (Colombia to the United States):

> [After a few academic experiences] I realized I had to be a professor. That was it. I didn't want to do anything else. And I knew that, to be a professor, and I knew that if I went back to Colombia, I was gonna live a poor life struggling with five jobs in five different universities and, you know, one class here, another class there. Because the academia in Latin America in general, at the time, was awful. Was badly paying, had no stability, no research. And all my professors either were professionals who taught classes by the side, they were Jesuits who had their life taken care of, or, the ones that were full-time professors, had three and four jobs in different universities and were, like, coming and going all the time. And I was like, "I don't want that. I've seen what my professors here in the U.S.—how they live. And, you know, they have a car, they own a house. That's what I want." And so, that's when I decided to stay.

Restrictive professional circumstances were also cited for universities in high-resource countries. For example, Evan (Belgium to Europe) explained, "At the university, even if I still think it's a very good university, the opportunities for growth, both at the level of promotion [and] at the level of what you can simply do, were deeply problematic." Edith (New Zealand to the United Kingdom) deliberated for a long time for a choice between positions in two countries. In the end, she applied for a permanent job in the United Kingdom and got it: "I just kind of felt, 'I'd worked so hard for so long with so little, and suddenly, to have some job security again in a good institution,' I just felt like I couldn't pass it up. So I decided to stay."

Being recruited for prestigious positions later on in one's career was motivated by other professional reasons. For example, Amanda (United Kingdom to the United States) appreciated the opportunity to change to a more friendly work environment: "I think it's definitely better being an academic here than in the U.K. Way less surveillance. We would be often, at least once a week, having to report on something or other—research reports, teaching reports, track everything you are doing." What struck Doina (Romania to the United States) as symbolic of the professional opportunities that opened up to her with her move was the availability of resources:

> We were kind of starting to understand what a library here in the United States looks like. We still tell students, "You are so lucky that you have Academic Search and all of those resources. They would cost amounts that you would not be able to afford." And somebody in a country where they don't have these systems through the university, because the university is not rich enough to buy into such a program, people can't find these things. [. . .] Not easy to get information.

For Lars (the United States to Singapore), it was about his internal sense of ability to thrive. He explained, "I had a sweetheart job in the U.S. But I felt that you either move forward or you die. You don't really just stay stagnant. And I felt I would have been stagnant if I stayed. [. . .] I just felt that it was time to push myself and challenge myself. And I thought that, in particular, going to a different culture would really push me cognitively and stretch me a little bit."

Similarly, Vihaan (India to the United States) prioritized his desire to invest in scholarship:

> I have those romantic illusions that someday, you never know, I'll go back to India. Then again, I think on the more practical front, that's unlikely to happen. My parents would like me to go back and spend more time there or move back permanently. I would have all the family reasons to do that at some point in time. Professionally, I don't think I'll be able to do the kind of work I do, and the kind of things I really enjoy doing, back in India. There are a couple of very nice universities, but I think they're mostly still teaching-oriented universities, and at least the research side of things, which I do enjoy a lot, would not be as prominent if I were to move back.

Finding the right balance between research and teaching and being able to devote oneself to research was central in the decision-making process that Demetrios (Greece to the United States) went through:

> I didn't look anywhere else; I didn't look beyond the U.S. I think I felt that I had committed enough time and resources to figure things out in American academia and that I owed it to myself to explore that option more. Plus, my sense was, and I don't think I was wrong, that academics in the U.S. have more opportunities to find resources to support their research agenda. And there's a healthier balance between teaching and research, and academic work is valued more. Not at the abstract or moral level, but, you know, as a market, as a professional you can do better for yourself than you would in most countries. It's a profession that is fairly respectable. But that respect doesn't translate in many countries into your ability to, you know, live a more comfortable life and, at the same time, really do what you want to do research-wise.

The ability not only to devote oneself to research but to do it according to Western norms of excellence played a role in Xiao's (China to the United States) decision. She explained,

> In the past few decades, universities in China are changing very rapidly. And a lot of things are very uncertain. And academic norms are transforming. For example, when you want to publish something

in a Chinese academic journal, a double-blind review is not the norm. That's something I really feel uncomfortable with. [...] I really felt uncomfortable with promotion procedures and so on. The criteria are not clearly spelled out and sometimes it is not at all fair. I don't feel comfortable working there unless I can see everything that's expected is clearly laid out and I know what to work for. [...] I still research China, so sometimes I think that things in China can change. But I don't really want to go back to China.

Thus, professional considerations included not only financial benefits but also the ability to do research, academic freedom, and rigorous academic norms.

Political Reasons

Political considerations were a broad category that included the cultural and social context as well. These consisted of the third group of reasons for immigration that impacted personal motivations and decision-making. For some, it was an uncomfortable environment, as shared by Demetrios, a gay interviewee (Greece to the United States): "Same-sex rights in Europe, in Greece, are a bit different than they are here. So from a personal standpoint, I'm better off living here, in the U.S., and in certain areas of the U.S." Evan (Belgium to Europe) added politics to a list of reasons that pushed him to move around: "They have to do with the changing political configuration in Belgium, which became much more nationalist and right-wing. Making it uncomfortable, and basically, pretty sad as a living environment."

Yerim (South Korea to the United States) expressed her discomfort with the general environment in her home country in response to a question about staying in the United States if she had a job offer in Korea. She said, "I love my country, I love people there [in Korea], but I do not like the organization of lives there. How people work and how the organizational relationship, because of the authorities and the strict ways of doing things. I don't know that I would want to work at any organization, unless it's an Americanized organization where I don't have to experience the reverse culture shock of, you know, now I have to all of a sudden behave like a Korean. Then I just can't."

Several interviewees mentioned transformative events that served as their "aha" moments. Such was the case of Brexit for moves away from the United Kingdom, and earlier, the politics of the Thatcher government, as shared by Patrick (Scotland to Belgium): "I had a Swedish girlfriend at the time, and after two years we had planned to move back to England and I would go back teaching and she would be a student. And that year Margaret Thatcher, who became prime minister, tripled the fees for overseas students, which meant we couldn't afford to go. So that one act of the Thatcher government began, and changed my life completely. And so, I stayed in Sweden."

Paula (Germany to the United Kingdom) was one of the interviewees who was contemplating moving away from the United Kingdom after many years there, following Brexit:

> Basically, the decision was made with the Brexit referendum three years ago; we thought we'd better get ready. We bought a house seven years ago in London and we thought, "What happens if Brexit comes along and we're not able to sell our house but we need to move to Germany?" [...] One of the reasons, apart from our parents, why we wanted to actually sell our house in London was we were really upset. We feel European, and we were both so upset that Britain wanted to leave Europe, that we felt that, okay, in that case, you know, we don't want to be here anymore [with the] feeling of being rejected as Europeans. Even though London is a bubble, it's a cosmopolitan city, it still felt like "Hmm, you know, I don't necessarily really want to be in this country anymore."

Another example of disillusion was related by Leo Yin (China to the United States): "I might have had a good career in China. But I don't regret changing my career. The main reason was, really, 1989. 'Cause we were all involved in the student movement in '89. I was also already being exposed to social theory, Western social theory. After the 1989 Student Movement, Chinese academia was hit hard. I had friends and students, you know, who quit academia and went into business. [They had] a lot of disillusionment." The political environment in China remained a concern for other interviewees even more recently, as the following example presented by Ning (China to the United States) demonstrated. In response to my question of what attracted her to the United States, she responded, "Probably the freedom. Freedom or liberty." Later in the interview, she elaborated on how the political restrictions in China are still impacting her work presently (e.g., the surveillance of her curriculum vitae and PowerPoint presentation when she visits): "People can say whatever they want to say in private, but as long as you do not make public announcement... [...] I don't want to cause trouble for myself and my family. [...] My mother always says, 'Oh, if it were during the cultural revolution, what you just said could make you arrested.' People are traumatized by that. Especially the Chinese government of now. He [President Xi Jinping] worships Mao. He is taking China back to the cultural revolution."

Several of the interviewees left the country of their birth given the political conflict in which it was immersed. Dana (Israel to the United States) shared,

> Leaving the post-Oslo bloodbath had to do with my choosing to leave Israel. I was living in Tel Aviv. It was a time of heightened alert. We just, every other day, you could have buses exploding and, you know, I was riding my scooter and I would try to stay away from city buses. And my sister was working at a bookstore right across from the big terror attack that happened at the big synagogue. And my boyfriend at the time—now husband—was taking the bus every day. It was really terrifying. It felt like it was a Russian roulette. With that happening, and also this feeling of disillusionment about collective action politically... [...] I feel like that really put a lot of steam behind my decision to pursue higher education in the United States.

Echoes of the impact of the Israeli-Palestinian conflict and the resulting political climate were cited by other participants who moved from Israel to the United States. Another narrative from an unresolved conflict situation came from Anna (Cyprus/Greece to the United Kingdom), a daughter to immigrant parents who spent her earlier life witnessing the Greek-Turkish conflict on the island (related in chapter 2), and spending much time in both Cyprus and Greece, explained,

> In many ways, I had a dual identity of being inside and outside, and being Cypriot and Greek has always been part of my reality. And this came with a sense of comfort, of being able to live in different places, but also with anxieties sometimes of not belonging. So, I always knew that, as soon as I finished school, I would go. Because I felt, "Cyprus is a small place. It's even smaller because of the politics of war and nationalism. I'm out of here as soon as I get the chance." The fact that I always thought I

would be a migrant myself. And always—even at times of, you know, personal difficulty, moving on—it became a way to find my way in the world, in a way. So, it was like, "Okay, what's my next destination now."

In addition to political circumstances that pushed some of my interviewees away, a few who were political activists decided to leave because they felt they would not be given a fair chance to flourish in their home countries. For example, Gaus (Pakistan to the United States) shared, "I'm involved in a lot of social activism. So kind of advocating for democracy reform. I advocated for LGBTQ rights using Twitter and Facebook. Things like these. And suddenly, like, we've been in Pakistan and they started like, to crack down on it more. [. . .] So the major concern was freedom of speech, the freedom to express myself, and the security. And then the career options."

Hassan (Iran to the United States), who immigrated decades earlier, and under different circumstances, related,

> I was in trouble politically. I was very active politically during my undergraduate and graduate studies in Iran at the time under the Shah. I was arrested several times and all this stuff in Tehran [. . .] so I was practically forced to leave Iran, and the only avenue that I had was to pursue my Ph.D., so I could leave, and then wait to see what happens in Iran. [. . .] While I was studying, a revolution happened in Iran, and I got very excited, and I got ready to go [. . .] but then, while I was in the process of getting ready to go, things started changing in the whole revolution in Iran. It started getting an Islamic flavor, which was completely not in my way of thinking. I never thought it was going to be the Islamic Republic of Iran [. . .] and after a year, after I saw all these dramatic changes occurring in Iran, I decided— "No, this is not going to be my way. I cannot live in that society." So I stayed here and decided I was going to be an American.

While the above examples originated in Islamic societies, Antonio (Puerto Rico to the mainland United States) was affected by the consequences of his activism under completely different circumstances:

> Well, little did I know that my pro-independence advocacy during my college years was going to face the wall of political discrimination. The centrist government had changed, and it was now a right-wing

government in Puerto Rico. I was told many years later that the president of the university informed the director of the School of Journalism where I was supposed to go back to work when I finished my degree, that he didn't want any more pro-independence professors there. And I didn't get a job anywhere in Puerto Rico, no matter how much I tried. But no tears on that because with such a great degree and all the research that I had learned to do and the type of analysis that I was doing with studies of media and Latinos in the United States, I got a tenure-track job in 1982 at a West Coast U.S. university.

Sometimes, the drive to move away from one country was less dramatic politically and more subtle. For example, Florence (the United States to Canada) shared,

> I think I always, ever since I worked—I don't know. You know, when I was studying political science, I've always felt like country borders are highly problematic things that create nationalism, exceptionalism in the sense of the United States, xenophobia, just so many problems. And I never really saw myself as an American first when I was traveling in the world. I saw myself as a person you know, who was relating to other people in the world. So, the United States—I can't stand the exceptionalism rhetoric, and I cringe whenever I hear some senator or somebody from the president's office talking about how America is such an exceptional and great country 'cause, you know, I had seen other exceptional and great countries and exceptional people. So, I was very happy to get away from that, and Canada isn't—they don't have that kind of exceptionalism rhetoric. And I, you know, I'm a big believer in social democracy, and Canada was more that.

While the above events served to push academics away from their countries, there were also examples of pull forces to immigrate. Similar to my own story, the election of Barack Obama to the presidency of the United States in 2008 was referenced in several of the interviews, as creating a sense of hope and cementing a decision to stay in the United States for those already toying with the idea. Richard (Australia to the United States) recalled this event: "I vividly remember the night Obama was elected. I was on a flight back from Europe, and normally the flights are quiet and subdued, and on this one people were jumping and dancing in the aisles with excitement, feeling there was a new dawn in America—I never experienced anything like this on a flight before. The sheer elation of people on the plane, and I remember feeling happy to go back to the U.S."

An example from a Central American country being attracted to the American Midwest was provided by Daniela (Colombia to the United States):

> The pressure of working in this NGO and being afraid all the time, we would go to restaurants and whisper. Like, my friends and I, at some point, we realized, "Why are we whispering?" And it's because we were afraid all the time. So, compare that to getting on this bus and going on this beautiful windy road—it's fall, fall in Ohio—with the, you know, the hills and the trees and everything. [...] I never saw a weapon in town; I don't think I ever saw the police. Or at least, maybe the police, but the military? The military? No. [...] And you know, hippies are walking around and everyone is like, "Hi, how are you doing?" in the street. And the cobblestone streets. I was like, "What the hell is this? Like, where am I?" I loved it. I couldn't care less if I belonged or didn't or whatever. It was like, "Ah. I can breathe. I can, you know, I don't have to be afraid all the time." I mean, I realized then the level of constant fear that I had internalized living in Colombia. And so, I loved it.

The 3Ps—personal, professional, and political drivers behind immigration—continued to play a role throughout my participants' careers and resurfaced when I later in the interview discussed with them the possibility of returning to their country of origin. We will return to that theme later on in the book.

The Path of Graduate Studies

The most common path of immigration, and especially to the United States and the United Kingdom, was one through graduate studies that eventually led to an academic career in the new country. Many of the participants chose to complete their Ph.D. studies in the United States or the United Kingdom without necessarily planning to stay there after graduation. As they got accustomed to the academia and culture in these countries, evaluated the potential benefits professionally and personally of staying there, got gradually disconnected from their home country, and put themselves on the "academic job market," opportunities opened up, they accepted positions offered to them, and they stayed. This narrative repeated itself to many of the participants, moving from different countries. Some of the interviewees embarked on their graduate studies journey convinced that they would go back once they were done, but things changed during the path and often serendipity got in the way of earlier plans. For example, Mayur (India to the United States) shared how that transition occurred in his case:

> The plan was to actually go back to India. Which was, I still remember, it was definitely the plan in my first year, maybe a little bit in the second year also. At some point during my second-year stay, I think that's where it started kind of changing. And I think, maybe by the end of my second year, it was clear that there was a good possibility I would actually stay here instead of going back to India. At the end of my second year I visited India—and that was my first time going back to India since I came to study—and realizing that almost unknowingly or subconsciously I kind of, I don't know, shifted the culture. So the same culture in India was now a little bit foreign to me, and I kind of started thinking, oh man, now I don't fit in here as much as well. And I could see that the more time I spent away from India, this was going to just keep getting harder. And that's what actually happened. That I found myself not fitting as well in the same culture.

Nathan (Israel to the United States) also experienced a change of plans during his studies that he did not anticipate in advance:

> When I came to do my Ph.D. at [an East Coast U.S. university] my clear intention was "I'm going to get a Ph.D. I'm going to do it about media therapy and teaching and come back to Israel with my degree. I will open a school, you know, and do the vision that I wanted to do." Very shortly after, it was clear to me that that was not going to be the path and that things were evolving and changing. Seeing what my advisor was doing and understanding that I needed to shift my understanding and that maybe there is a different path to where I want to get.

Similarly, Gaus (Pakistan to the United States) explained: "The plan was, I would tell my friends, 'We are going to go back because our country needs us and this and that.' But like for the first two years, I didn't have any plans of staying in the U.S. after the Ph.D. But in the end, my plans changed."

Iracema (Brazil to Portugal) originally moved for a one-year master's program, but her decision not to return had major implications for her personal life as well:

> So, I came to spend this year here, and my husband stayed in Brazil. It was really hard for us. So, I started to work on this project, and then things changed because I started to like to live here. I made friends. I started to think about the possibility of staying here. So, when my husband came here once to visit me for a month—it was not that good. And when I went to Brazil at the end of the year, when I entered my home, I thought, "This is not my home anymore." I don't know. I think I was different. I was like, "Half of me wants to stay here. The other part wants to stay there." And I was not very sure. But I did—I applied for a Ph.D. scholarship, and then I got the Ph.D. So, I got divorced; it changed my whole life. And I came here to live."

The decision not to go back represented to some a major transformation in self-perception, well beyond a career choice. Such was the case of Maya (Israel to the United Kingdom), who shared,

> The plan was very clearly to go back after we were done studying. You know, I'm a granddaughter of two Zionist pioneers who were among the founders of the kibbutz in Israel. We're coming from a lineage of a very patriotic family. My father was in a top unit in the army. We were very much the kind of the "salt of the land" type. And I also always felt, and still do, in many ways, very attached to Israel as a place—to its culture, and friends. I didn't entertain thinking about not going back. About staying in the U.K. It was still under the kind of, you know, an umbrella of a "temporary" stay when I extended it for my Ph.D. and then longer . . .

Others went abroad from the start with a lack of conviction one way or another, open to seeing where the circumstances would take them. For example, Jose (Argentina to the United States) shared: "I was toying with the idea of studying abroad. I liked my life in Argentina, but, you know, I was curious about experiencing life somewhere else. So, I came to do my Ph.D. [...] I didn't come up with the idea that I was going to return. I was like, 'We'll see what happens.'"

Similarly, Rumia (India to the United States) had an open mind about the future:

> I was starting to get interested in studying mass communication in the United States because I wanted to go in that direction. And, you know, in India at the time, there weren't enough programs. So I applied here. What made it a very sort of a normal thing to do was, I already had family and friends who were studying here. So, it seemed like, a very doable thing and people do that. And it didn't feel like a huge first step, in a way. My father has already done it in the past. And other members of the family had. [...] When I left, I was in two minds [of whether I was going to stay or go back]. I was like "I'm gonna see what happens" [...] and I have been always very lucky that my parents are very supportive in helping me make decisions and do what I was good at and what they felt also I would thrive in. And if that meant going somewhere else, as long as I maintained connections and all, they'd be fine with that.

Many of the stories highlighted the mentorship and support of individual professors who saw the potential in the interviewee and offered encouragement, advice, and very important fellowships and assistantships. While these stories cannot be retold in detail without breaking the commitment to confidentiality, they were prominent, and the retelling of the immigration story also relayed the interviewee's deep sense of gratitude.

Reactions to Immigration

Family and friends' reactions to the migration decision depended to a large degree on the general cultural attitudes toward mobility, national identity, and the value associated with professional aspirations. Many were supportive—or at least did not express strong objections. Examples abound. Gisela (Germany to the United States) related: "They always thought it was great. They always told me they're very proud. And my mom especially. [...] She just thinks I'm sort of a miracle child to have survived [leukemia] and she thinks whatever I do is awesome. She just has this pure mother's pride and just loves whatever I do." Juha (South Korea to the United States) explained: "My mom and dad always said, 'Do whatever you want to do.' I mean, they already have kind of global mindset. [...] My mom said, 'It's okay; I do not want us to be a burden on you.' That kind of thinking. They always let me do what I want to do." Avi (Israel to the United States) related, "My parents were always supportive. My father, unfortunately, passed away, but my mom was always supportive of that because she wanted us to try and accomplish the best we can." Parents wishing the best for their children and not trying to stand in their way was a motif that returned again and again in the narratives of the participants.

In a few cases, these aspirations were also motivated by a realization of the limitations of what the home country can offer, and being very proud of the opportunities their children had abroad. Such, for example, was the case of Gaus (Pakistan to the United States), who explained, "It's like a sign of success and accomplishment because getting an education from the U.S. is a big thing. And everyone was like 'Okay, so you will succeed in getting something that no one in our family could.'" Armin (Barbados to the United States) also framed parental attitudes in a more general national interpretation: "I think all the parents of my generation, probably still now, feel that it is a necessary journey. And that it is, around the poorer classes, that traveling abroad is something that was highly desired."

Friends, too, were supportive in many cases, as Griet (Belgium to the United States) related: "In general, friends were very supportive. My best friends go, 'I can't believe you're leaving me.' But, you know, people are supportive and kind of find it fun to follow through our Facebook what's going on here and whatever." Others recognized the benefit that their move offered to their friends, as did Iracema (Brazil to Portugal): "My mom, she loves to travel. She always said to me, 'Go, it's so good.' She never said, 'Oh, I miss you.' She is very happy that I am here. And my friends, they love it, because they have an apartment to stay in when they visit."

In some cases, concerns over the reaction from university colleagues turned into a heartwarming surprise. Jozef (Belgium to the United

States), who immigrated at the prime of his career, shared the moving send-off he received from his university colleagues:

> I was kind of worried that they would react badly. But they gave me a farewell party you'd usually give someone upon retirement. It must have cost a lot of money because it was in a fancy place with food and drinks and a lot of people showed up. I felt as if I went to my funeral, in a sense, 'cause it was so wonderful. It was really supportive. I hadn't expected that. [...] There were a couple of people I think I made uncomfortable because I made them realize, "I could do this too." Or, you know, "Why have I never considered this?" I got a few of those reactions. But the university showed itself, I mean, its nice side. [...] And so, that's a relief. That's been really liberating. They reacted as a family, and I didn't expect that. So, they were very supportive.

Jozef's experience resonated so strongly with my own "farewell party" from Tel Aviv University, which was a full-day symposium on the development of feminist studies in Israel with multiple presentations from former Ph.D. students and colleagues, intercepted with personal congratulatory speeches. I felt like Jozef that I had the privilege and good fortune to hear the obituaries that could have possibly been said at my funeral. What an uplifting experience that still gives me shivers of warm emotions when I think of it or browse through the photos and written notes from the event.

Not all of the participants encountered full-hearted support. Many had to struggle with less positive reactions. Some parents and friends were frowning over the decision for ideological reasons and/or a personal sense of loss. Most had mixed reactions, as expressed by Amanda (the United Kingdom to the United States): "I think they were probably a bit sad. But also excited. At this point both my parents were still alive and they were very excited. They thought it was great that one of our family was going to America. [...] I think my daughter especially was sad, but excited by the idea that they could come and visit." Meena (India to the United States) feels very emotional sharing this heartache:

> It was my grandmother. She cried so much when I left. Because I was her closest person and I was her caregiver. She's fifty years older than

me. But she was such a selfless person that she was like, "I want you to have a good life. I don't want to hold you back." You know. "So, you should go and make a life for yourself." And we would talk on the phone and so on, but it's not the same thing. But she never asked me to come back. And she always felt, if that's where you're happy, then that's where you should be. The only pressure I faced from my family was to have kids. So. They kept insisting and they said, "Send them back to us! We'll look after them. Just pop them out."

Clearly, having children was seen as a hopeful path for familial continuity and contact.

Some parents saddened by the separation were more forceful and direct in expressing their disappointment and pain, as Jennifer (the United Kingdom to the United States) expressed: "My father says, 'you should move back. We need you here.' [. . .] I am the one who changes the light bulb, you know . . ." Lynn (the United States to Europe) deals with difficult emotional pressure that has not eased over time:

> My family was heartbroken. [. . .] My mom still cries. My father was scared but proud. And the rest of my siblings felt like I was abandoning them. [. . .] It was awful for them. [. . .] They feel that the longer I've been there, the more European I am and feel like I am changing. They always tell me I'm more proper. I think I'm just more mature. [. . .] And I'll say, "Right, I'm heading home now" and my mom, she's like "That's not your home; that's where you live right now." And it upsets them.

A sense of betrayal, perhaps similar to my own experience in the opposite direction (leaving Israel to the United States), was expressed by Eddy (Europe to Israel):

> My mother, my siblings didn't like that. We are a European family in the sense that nobody immigrated for two or three generations. [. . .] And I also married a foreigner, so it is mixed because she was very Catholic. My mother felt betrayed. She was very angry that I moved to Israel, and her grandchildren were not baptized and maybe will have to serve in the army. And on top of that the peace process collapsed in 2000 and there were all the terrorist attacks and it became a nightmare. So complicated, to put it in one word.

A different version of the sense of betrayal and disappointment was shared by Smita (India to the United States):

> My father was very opposed to my coming to the U.S. and did not support me. He was an incredibly loving, kind father. But it was on principle. He couldn't understand why, by the time I had come into academia, there were places for me to do a Ph.D. and study and live in India. He really didn't understand why I had to go to the U.S. [...] He was kind of like, "Why would you not stay here and help build your own country?" You know? I mean, "We need, the country needs you." So it was a very difficult decision.

Smita's struggle resonated strongly with my own sense of leaving Israel, as I described in the first chapter sharing my journey.

A different type of bewilderment over the immigration decision was related by Claire (Canada to the United States):

> They think I'm crazy. The public opinion in Canada of America is very low. Very, very low. So, you know, they all lump all Americans together into one group, and there aren't any particularly nice adjectives that I can come up with to describe what they think of them [... following the election of President Trump]. It definitely seems to them like most Americans are racist, ignorant, all those things.

In contrast to Jozef's party described above, in a few cases, colleagues resented the loss of key people, as suggested by Richard (Australia to the United States): "Well, the professional community didn't forgive me for fifteen years, because I was very much a recognized person in that profession. I'm not being unkind, you know, in saying that they were not forgiving. They expressed a kind of a loss, although I've gone back to Australia many times to do my work."

Self-Reflection

Whatever mixture of personal, professional, and political motivations for immigrating, my interviewees described their transitions as sometimes a consequence of deliberate thinking and choice, sometimes "inertia" and in many ways, privileged opportunities that came their way in serendipity. Many had several stops around the world on the way to their final destination (for now). They had fellowships, such as Fulbright, and occasional temporary jobs. Others went directly from the Ph.D. to a tenure-track position. They highly valued the transformative process they have gone through by relocating, as expressed by Jon (the United Kingdom to the United States):

> You've got to have an adventure. You've got to transform yourself and reenergize yourself. And that aspect, how moving country and jobs makes you simultaneously re-evaluate yourself, I find it to be one of the most exciting things. That everything is reenergized by that. Having to learn everything new. So I deeply value that. It's been a privilege.

Similarly, Cosmas (Nigeria to the United States) explained: "I like exploring. I don't consider myself somebody to be confined to one country. I've always seen myself at the international level." Patrick (Scotland to Belgium) emphasized serendipity in his narrative: "I was lucky... There has never been a career plan. There has never been a clear path. I've always gone—I won't say I've gone with the wind exactly, but it's been a lot of opportunities. Always been a lot of situational factors, a lot of totally random events and decisions."

However, not everyone found peace and full acceptance of their new life. With some it remained a dilemma, as expressed by Constantinos (Greece to the United States), who admitted that not everyone was supportive of his decision to leave, which resonated with his own torn feelings:

> I think there was a little bit of resentment, like, a lot of friends from high school, they're like, okay, now you're American, and you don't care anymore, which is not true. I care very much and want to help Greece. But you know, it's a very complicated situation. It's a dual identity thing, and it can be challenging at times. I'll always consider myself Greek. And nothing will change that no matter what.

While the physical voyage to the new country may have ended, the open-ended questions about lasting challenges and identity issues are the topics of our next two chapters.

4

The Challenges

Why Is Immigration
So Difficult?

"It Just Kind of Mounted Up"

Once in the new host country, whether for a few years or many, these academic immigrant colleagues settled into a life characterized by dealing with the tensions of two simultaneous adaptation processes: inward integration (i.e., preservation of family unity and shared cultural denominator, transmission to children and family, and community consolidation) and outward integration (i.e., social and cultural integration into their new institutional surroundings and the host society-at-large).[1] A further complication is that these two processes complement as well as contradict one another as the immigrant academic moves, constantly, between different social and cultural spheres. To succeed in these demanding and challenging processes, interviewees and their families needed to maximize the use of the resources at their disposal (e.g., cultural knowledge, linguistic abilities, social networking, financial means, etc.), including their professional networks and scholarly expertise.

From their responses, as well as my own experiences, it seems that the tensions involved in this complex process never seem to cease, even after decades of life in a host country. In many ways, living a "double life" becomes a distinctive feature of their existence. For example, there are constant reminders of "otherness," such as linguistic challenges; common questions about accents; mispronunciation of their names; the familiar "where are you from" questions; encountering "black holes" in corridor conversations about culture, politics, sports, and trivia; and saying "the wrong thing" as a result of cultural insensitivity.[2]

While this experience is shared by immigrants more generally and is not unique to academics, my focus here is on the inward and outward integration processes within academic institutions as well as the implications for developing a sense of home and belonging through their workplace and professional experiences. While the ideals of diversity, equity, and inclusion are not necessarily shared across the United States, not to mention globally, they were very much on the mind of most interviewees, who were lamenting their longing for a sense of a holistic home, where inward and outward were integrated, where they felt "whole."

My interviewees' experiences were by no means homogenous. Many variables impacted their sense of belonging: the circumstances of their immigration, whether they had married or partnered with a member of the host society, the country (and in the case of the United States, the specific state) they were living in, institutional policies, colleagues they encountered, and naturally, their personality characteristics. It is possible to group their stories of institutional integration into the following themes that emerged in their responses to my questions about the challenges they encountered. They focused on the transitions and "culture shock" experiences, the ongoing challenges in culture and academia, and specifically on what they perceived as racist encounters, gender discrimination, and intersectional biases.

Transition Challenges

Most of the participants had stories to share about their adjustment period to the new host country. Many of their accounts were full of self-deprecating humor, others bitter and painful, but all cited the culture shock that was part of the transitional period. Meena's (India to the United States) reflexive narrative of her transition as a graduate student integrates many of these elements—cultural, technical, academic, and very personal:

> When you get ripped out of your comfort zone and the context where everything makes sense and the world makes sense, even if you

dislike various aspects of it, and you get thrown into a different world where you have to relearn and understand how even the most basic thing, such as how do you get money? The idea of an ATM was bewildering. The idea is that you would have a little card and you put it into some machine, and it gives you money. It was . . . [laughter] It was just shocking. This little university town that I just could not believe where I was. And then, you get thrown into a classroom situation where, you know, you're trying to navigate various hurdles and figure out how to make sense of all of this.

Cultural shock is truly a traumatic experience because your whole identity is erased and, you know, even little things you were known for, like, "I make really good tea," nobody knows that about me here, or even values it. Or wants to have the kind of tea that I make. Because it's not their fault; it's just that they don't know that and it's not part of their culture. So, it was challenging. And the other part is after having strived and dreamed of coming to America, now you land here and it's just like, "Whoa. This is so scary." There's, you can't, there's no option to fail because I couldn't go back to India.

So, no matter how much hardship, trauma, depression, or whatever one went through, you just had to push through. There was no time to reflect on the fact that maybe I don't belong here. Or, I should be doing something else. No, you have to do well in your studies. Have to get As in everything because that's how you survive in this country. [. . .] And I don't think I have the vocabulary even to be able to put into words what those experiences were. I mean, emotional intelligence is not something we're all necessarily born with. You learn it as you grow older. So . . .

Several participants recalled very concrete incidences that symbolized significant cultural differences and the essence of the transition. Avi (Israel to the United States) presents such an example, humorously:

It was a transition on many levels. You know, a big one was the weather. I never saw a whole lot of ice and snow before coming here. [. . .] I remember one morning it was frozen, and I did not realize that I didn't know what black ice meant. I was just crossing from the dormitories across the street to the school, and I slipped all over the main street. Luckily, I did not get hit by anybody. And then, the security officer over at the school came over rushing, picked me up, and said, "What happened?" I said, "I have no idea what happened. What is this?" He says, "This is ice." I said, "ice?" I never saw this before. So that was kind of one element there.

A very different moment of realization of the experience of culture shock was related by Armin (Barbados to the United States):

> Well, that was a very interesting experience for me. I think I had one moment of what I would call culture shock. When I was sitting in the student lounge, and watching the news. A student came in and turned the knob or the channel to some kind of soap opera or something. To me, it was just, I couldn't believe it. Because we'd be reared so much on following international events from the time I was in elementary school. To me, it stood out as being extraordinary, not only strange but violently assertive.

Rhi Won (South Korea to the United States) focused on the cultural differences that were so bewildering to her and difficult to adjust to, including issues of privacy and physical distance, as well as respect toward the elderly:

> When I came to the States by myself, everything was totally different and unfamiliar. Language, culture, and even different ethnic people around me [. . .] and everything is big in size. For example, even McDonald's small-sized Coke is much bigger than the one in Korea. And everyone around me spoke English. No one understood my background and culture much. [. . .] For example, distance, and privacy. In Korea, privacy or space between people was not very important. But in the U.S., I had to pay attention to individual privacy or space between people. For example, when using the ATM, in the U.S. people who are about to use the machine wait with enough distance beyond the one who is currently using it. But in Korea, some people are standing right behind you. So, they don't intentionally give others some private space. [. . .]
> Also in other areas . . . sometimes Korean people tend to ask too private questions, such as, are you married? How much money are you

making? It's cultural differences. Korea is a more collective society than America. In Korea, age matters because we have different language levels for different age groups. Here in the United States, it's OK for me to call you "Dafna," even though I am much younger than you, right? In Korea, I have to call you "Dr. Dafna" with respect because I am younger and you are a professor. So in Korea, we have very polite ways of calling older people or people who are in higher social positions. To figure out who is older or who is socially higher in a position, Korean people tend to ask a lot of private questions to people who are new to them.

The central role of religion in U.S. society was quite a surprise for several of my interviewees (including myself), as suggested by Gisela (Germany to the United States): "Very shocking. It was the complete opposite because I grew up without religion being a thing. Right? I didn't even know anything about it. I wouldn't even identify as an atheist, having made a conscious decision. It just didn't play a role in East German systems for the most part."

There are so many taken-for-granted aspects of life in each culture that become visible once one moves to a different environment. George (Romania to the United States) shared a host of other adjustments he had to make that made him reflect on broader cultural differences:

> I was startled when I came here and then, for the first time, I became the owner of a house where I had to cut the grass. Before coming to [a major midwestern city], I never cut the grass in my life. So, I had to buy a mini-tractor mower because the grass field around the house is so big. You can't do it with a push-mower. So, then I asked myself, "Why are these people investing so much money in keeping the grass and then cutting the grass instead of using the ground to produce something?" That's how we were told in Romania: grow some flowers; grow some fruit trees; grow some tomatoes, some cucumbers, something that will feed your family, and you have something to do around the house. Do not cut the grass and collect the leaves. [...]
>
> Here, you have to be mild-mannered. Otherwise, you sound like you are cringing. And if somebody were to call the police on you, then it could turn out bad. I don't have any qualms, but I'm trying to keep it nonjudgmental. I also realized what were the bad things in my culture, from my country of origin. Meaning a little bit of the

perception that the world is smaller. That's a good thing for the Americans, that they think the whole world is their playground. I mean, it's a different style.

Even moving from one English-speaking culture to another one was surprisingly challenging, as Anne (Canada to the United Kingdom) and her husband found out: "And it was anything from easy, aside from the accents and all of that. We just didn't know how anything worked. Like the bank. Needing to buy a plug separately for a cassette player and wire it yourself. There were just little things like that. You know, we just kept stumbling into really difficult things [...] and it just kind of mounted up. And we felt really, this is hard."

Whether it referred to sliding over black ice, managing the ATM, not knowing how close to stand when speaking to a colleague, or having to mow the lawn, the term "culture shock" was often invoked by the participants during the interviews when discussing their transitions into a new host country.

Ongoing Challenges

Transitions into a new host country challenge most immigrants. However, while immigrants are supposedly integrated and enjoying successful professional and personal lives, most of their difficulties remain ongoing, even after many years of living in the new country. Remaining a stranger to the culture, feeling as "other," may ease over time, but it does not go away, it seems, ever. Jose (Argentina to the United States), a well-established academic scholar and leader, expressed it clearly:

> I go through the motions of everyday life that you do in terms of the American lifestyle. But I always feel the absence of something that is not there. The type of social connection, the type of work connection. So, I step a little bit outside of my home, which is my house, you know, my family, I go outside, and it feels very—it's strange because it's, it's familiarly foreign. Because I know it, because I've been living here for thirty-plus years, but it's not me. It's not—it doesn't fully capture who I am. So, that's what reminds me periodically that I'm from somewhere else. So, the way people interact with each other, the kind of relationships people develop, what it means to be a man in America, which is very different from being a man in

Argentina—being a colleague is very different, and being a friend is very different. I mean, so, almost every single role is very different. And I'm sort of, in the abstract, well-integrated. Right? In the sense that, you know, my kids are Americans, I guess, and we have an American lifestyle and . . . but beyond that, it reminds me much of what my grandparents used to say about being an immigrant. They were perfectly, you know, functional in Argentine society. But they were not, let's say, Argentines.

Similarly, Eva (Brazil to Sweden), who also was well integrated, on the face of it, retained her sense of otherness, as she related,

I feel quite well integrated and I have a job and friends and then the family. And I understand the culture codes. But it's still—I, I would say I'm an integrated outsider. [. . .] I always look at the culture and social codes as an outsider. Things are not natural for me. [. . .] One is the thing with irony. Irony and sarcasm. The other thing is with lack of spontaneity. Like, just everything needs to be booked in advance. Everything needs to be planned. And I think that's the biggest difference.

Given that many of the interviewees moved to the United States, a lot of the examples related to that particular culture, at a turbulent time of the Trump presidency. Armin (Barbados to the United States), whom we just met above, moved to broader issues as the conversation unfolded:

Because I think everything I've written has been from a point of view that I don't understand. I don't understand the United States. I don't understand its contemporary politics. I don't understand how it sustains a president like the one it has now [Trump, at the time of the interview]. I am totally convinced that this—if we had the same leader in the Caribbean or somewhere else, that leader would have been gone by a democratic process. So, so, when I wrote about race, I didn't understand race either. So, I've always felt like I live in this country. I enjoy what I do. I like the people I like. I like the students I work with. But I fundamentally don't understand it. I don't understand it around health care. I don't understand it around education. And I don't understand the loyalty to very problematic projects within the working classes from the elites. I don't understand why political elites continue to pursue racial politics in the way that they do when I think they could actually procure political results by a different model.

The role of racial relationships in the U.S. culture seemed to be an area of confusion and bewilderment to other participants. Avi (Israel to the United States) expressed sentiments that I share as well, given our similar background:

> The other thing that is true for us, coming from a different country, is that we're not very aware of race relations. I couldn't make sense of that. Why do people make some sort of comments and so forth, I had no experience with any of that stuff. [...] So I'm still surprised, and I think a lot of it is because of the lack of transparency. In Israel everything is always transparent, you know. You kind of know what to expect. Here there are layers upon layers and layers, and that is hidden by things that I'm not privy to, like racial relationships and racial tensions. [...] And I was even surprised when, you know, my colleagues tell me there's anti-Semitism on campus. I said, "Really? Where?" There is. I just did not pay attention to it. [...] And I think it's navigating that. So, for example, being very careful about what you say, okay, and all that kind of stuff is something that takes time to adjust to.

Many other aspects of American culture and ways of being led my interviewees to feel they see things that others may not. Lillian (Canada to the United States) talked specifically about some key culturally contested areas in the United States:

> Something like gun laws I cannot understand, why we don't have gun laws. [...] For me, it feels like such a marker of distinction that I could never completely be on terms with what that means for people who don't, who support no reform. Similar to female reproductive rights. Similar to maternity leave. This, you know, kind of treatment of women in the workplace. And, of course, with the current administration. So, to me, there are moments where I feel more Canadian than ever, and where I want to tell people that I'm Canadian.

Differing styles of interpersonal relationships, too, created challenges mentioned by several of the interviewees. For example, Demetrios (Greece to the United States) reflected,

> I feel like there's this level of superficiality and, or lack of follow-up in interpersonal relationships that I can't quite get over. I don't know; I haven't quite put my finger on it. It's just apparent that I noticed, with people, that they don't form very strong long-term bonds that they're committed to. That may be just my experience; I don't know that that's a cultural trend. But yeah, I have very few, like, native-born American friends. Maybe it's because, also, in many cases, their sense of the world is very different from mine. It's all about the U.S. and viewing the world through that lens, and they have a hard time relating to other ways of looking at the world. Where it's something about, you know, an Italian or a Spaniard that has had to move to the U.S. and has had to deal with some of the similar issues that maybe I have at some level. And that creates a common set of references that translates across linguistic and cultural barriers. Where Americans who are born here and are native-born don't quite understand.

Nathan (Israel to the United States) encountered difficulties adjusting to the American interactional style, coming from the Israeli *dugri* penchant for direct speech.[3] Being caught off guard, he realized in retrospect that he needed coaching to fit in:

> Culturally, and also being in New England, there were a lot of subtleties. Like there is a joke that I don't understand, a cultural reference that I don't get exactly. [. . .] I don't miss the aggressiveness and the stress and the toughness and the in-your-face kind of thing in Israel that has been very difficult for me since I was a young kid. . . . In Israel, I'm being seen as very European, kind of, like, very mellow, chill, very polite. And it was very interesting for me that, in the U.S. and especially in New England, I was seen as very aggressive and very assertive, and I was like, are you kidding me? Like, this is assertive for you? [. . .] So I had different encounters that I didn't know how to interpret. And thank god I had different people that helped me demystify what was going on there. And some bridges were burned, and I couldn't retrieve. [. . .] Either a sentence I said or an action I did

that was inappropriate from the other person's point of view, and I was an outcast.

As in the case of Emma (China to the United States), other interviewees discovered that small talk and norms of everyday conversation also differ across cultures, as scholarship in intercultural communication has found.[4]

> To be honest, I don't have many American friends. So, even when I'm in conversation with my U.S. colleagues or friends or, like, classmates or peers, it's really difficult to understand what they are talking about. Maybe you understand the word, but sometimes when they mention names, it's very cultural-specific things. Like, or jokes. I don't understand. I could just, like, be there and listening but without really engaging in their conversations. I feel like it's really difficult to engage in conversations like small talk, like casual chats with colleagues or friends.

The ongoing difficulties of fitting in described by the participants in this study are not unique and are typical to the immigration experience around the world. We turn now to more specific experiences of efforts to integrate into the academic world which are unique to this group.

Challenges in Academia

Academic worlds add another layer of structures, norms, and expectations from their faculty that exacerbate difficulties of fitting in, especially when compared with homeland academic institutions and environments. Several interviewees went so far as to claim they felt invisible, that they were not seen by their institutions. The participants had many stories to tell about these unexpected difficulties encountered in the academy. Nadya (Bulgaria to the United States) described several of these aspects:

> My first few years were really difficult because, I mean, the culture shock of moving from eastern Europe to California. Like, things were very different, and I didn't know anyone, and I didn't understand

American academia. It just took a year or two to figure out how it works and how things are different from our universities and everything like that, and then I felt excluded from a lot of things. Not because people were trying to exclude me, but because I didn't have a shared background that would allow me to fit in. I couldn't talk about, and I still can't, like, I still don't get American football. And at the university, this was a huge thing. So, everyone was always talking about football. I grew up with soccer; I still to this day have no idea what's so interesting about football . . . I have no idea. [. . .] And with things like that, the local culture, just big celebrities and things like that. There's some other stuff that everyone just grew up with and into and you're coming from the outside. [. . .] I didn't fit in because I didn't understand a lot of the background that people shared, and I didn't.

Smita (India to the United States) found American academia to be uncomfortable for her on many levels:

I always felt like an outsider to my own culture. Partly because of my family history. Partly my personality. I'm not a total conformist person. [. . .] But then, coming to the U.S.—it's a new feeling of outsiderness. Not understanding sort of the American standards of politeness, of boundaries. Office hours. When you are supposed to talk to professors about what? [. . .] And yes, there were times when, clearly, I had transgressed some boundaries, and, you know, asked for too much or revealed my insecurities too much to somebody. Or maybe I talked inappropriately at some time, you know. So, I did experience those feelings of what you want to call culture shock. [. . .] There were professors who did not have Indian women students or South Asian women students, right? And there is this idea that there's a docility . . . it didn't stop me from talking, and sharing. And I could sense a bit of surprise. "Oh, this is not what I expected." And there were times when perhaps I didn't get it right. And there was a sort of sharp rebuke. Or a put-down.

Relationships with colleagues, not only students, presented another set of challenges. George (Romania to the United States) expressed his reaction to challenges that framed him as a loner, even invoking racist stereotypes:

You know, our style is different. So, people cannot relate to that. I still, even in departmental meetings, cannot discuss what I eat and what I drink, though that's the small talk that is usually done even in academic environments, which is something appalling to me. I cannot still be educated into that kind of small talk. So, I would like to talk about politics or culture. I would like to talk about history or art. I would like to talk about some intellectual preoccupation of one kind or another. But it doesn't work. So, I'm still perceived as a kind of loner. I do not relate to many of my colleagues. There were some situations in which, even in my department, I was perceived as too much of a loner, or as too much of a control freak. [...] So, there is something there that even my colleagues cannot surpass. Those who still maybe see me as a vampire. Or a dark person from eastern Europe. After so many years, there is still some intolerance that some people cannot pass over. And it hangs on, and it's floating there.

Language and Interpersonal Interaction

Linguistic fluency is a key social and professional capital for life in academia: teaching, publishing research, and networking with colleagues—all require excellent mastery of the dominant language of the institution of higher education in the given country. Just getting by with a foreign language does not cut it; one needs to operate and compete with native language speakers. Maya (Israel to the United Kingdom) described this challenge:

> I've been working now for twenty years in this language [English], I think the language for me, it's such a huge thing, especially so during my master's. I just felt almost handicapped in terms of my capacity to articulate my ideas both in writing and orally because so much emphasis is also put on participation in the class. I felt hyperconscious that my English was far from perfect and was probably full of grammatical mistakes and so on. And I did everything I could. I took extracurricular courses for writing in academic English—speaking in academic English. I did, like, everything I could, and I remember I would read every article that we had to read for the class once for the content, for the argument, and then I would literally, like, try to emulate how—to understand how it's written and highlight new words and I still have it. I still have a huge folder with all the new words and connectives and I remember feeling really, deeply disadvantaged

about language. And thinking that it would kind of really have an impact on my performance, which it didn't. Also, obviously, I gave it to a professional proofreader and everything on every single piece. But I think that's something that has stayed with me for a while because I remember at least in the very first years, when I started working as a lecturer, I would send almost every slightly significant email to my English proofreader to go through. I was so conscious of English not being my first language.

The intricacies of language are crucial at all levels of academic life. Jennifer (the United Kingdom to the United States) describes the realization she had about the differences between British English and American English that can become a game-changer in one's promotion procedures. She explained:

> I think it took me a long time to figure out that you have to be able to boast a little bit in this country. Boasting just isn't done in the U.K., and I always worry when we go to the U.K. for letters for promotion—and everyone's experienced this with Jon [the United Kingdom to the United States]. When Jon says, "I think that's quite good," he means, "That's fantastic." Whereas here, if you say that's "quite good," that means that's "Not good." That sounds awful to me. And so, when I had to write my promotion narratives, the chair at the time said, "I'm going to translate this into American for you." And what that meant was, "You've got to do some boasting," which was very difficult for me. It just was a genre that I wasn't familiar with.

The issue of language and particularly accent as markers of identity and otherness were cited as prominent features of standing out. The familiar question "Where are you from?" even if asked out of well-intended curiosity and sincere interest reminded them constantly they are "from somewhere else." Collectively, interviewees felt that their names, accents, and language imperfections undermined their authority in the classroom and among their peers, as Mina (India to the United States) shared painfully: "I remember that I got a comment [on my student evaluation]. It said, 'Ask this bitch to learn my language before she comes to teach us.' [. . .] That hurt me a lot. [. . .] The statement sort of talked about the hegemony within our discipline, like,

'Who are you from a third-world to come and teach me this when you cannot speak my language?'" Different English accents—Indian versus American, as Mina above relates, or Canadian versus British, as Anne (Canada to the United Kingdom) below shares, is enough to be a source of negative "outing" of immigrants:

> When I got the job, people started then kind of questioning, "Well, why are you here?" not in a necessarily unfriendly way, but it was always calling you out. Like the minute you open your mouth and they hear your accent, "Oh, where are you from?" and it still happens to me almost daily. If I meet someone new, "Oh, you're not from here" and it's like, "Actually, I am. I lived here since 2003." So it's still called out.

The appropriate interpersonal communication with colleagues, students, and superiors and expectations were also not necessarily obvious, and often very different from what one was used to from the home country.

Relationships with Students

Bridging norms and expectations of home and host cultures can create discontent for or even conflicts with students, as Demetrios (Greece to the United States) stated: "Sometimes I don't quite understand what students expect. For example, grading in the Greek system [. . .] is pretty harsh and unforgiving. Professors . . . tend to be a bit more removed from their students, and interactions are a bit more formal. Professors don't try to be amusing in the classroom." Wael (Jordan to the United States) has encountered a similar dissonance:

> One of the things that confused me was how classes are taught in the States. Both as a TA and as a student. Because I came from a culture where, you know, the teacher is God up there. And he has, you know, the Bible in his hand. And he will write the test and you will live or die by their sword, sort of thing. And that is not the case in the States. Right? There is a back-and-forth, and there are arguments. There is talk within the class. You don't necessarily have to raise your hand to make a point. You know, it's much more relaxed. It took me a while to get used to it as a student. And it took me a while to get used to it as a

TA. I think it's better, but it's not easy to get used to this kind of new style of back-and-forth in education.

Yerim (South Korea to the United States), coming from a collectivist culture where women are taught not to stand out and remain deferential to men of authority, had to learn to adjust to the individualistic-competitive norms of American academia:

> And so, I remember having a conversation with my advisor who told me, "You know, you're really brilliant, you're very smart, but you need to—you shouldn't agree with me all the time." And he knew that I was thinking—I did have the critical thinking skills, but I wasn't expressing that. Because I was always like, "Yes. Like, you're right." Always kind of nodding and listening and accepting. And so, that's when I realized, "Oh, I need to get out of my super-Korean-ness and really try to act more like an American scholar." And I thought a lot about what that means, and I became more vocal. I became more expressive, honest, and straightforward. Even though I didn't change who I am, I have always been straightforward if I need to. But it just became easier over time.

Iracema (Brazil to Portugal) had to make the opposite transition of academic expectations: "Yes, I think moving here influenced me a lot. Especially in the relationship with the students. Because one of the most difficult things for me is the relationship in professional and formal situations. Because here in Portugal, people are very formal, in comparison to Brazil. They keep their distance. And, also, during the interactions with the students, they always use titles. And this is really hard for me because in Brazil I used to have very close relationships with my students." What is the norm in one culture is the opposite in another, so it requires of the academic immigrant sometimes a complete reset of their behaviors, even their self-image as a professional.

Working with graduate students brought with it another layer of difficulties, even for the very experienced academics. Richard (Australia to the United States) explained:

> Probably the biggest difference for me was learning the ingrained cultures of academia across the continents. You know, for example, the Ph.D. training is so vastly different here, that it took me a long time to

get my head around the notion of two years of formal coursework, examinations—I still balk at those. But, you know, in some ways learning the culture, those differences, was a little bit hard because as you engage, you are then constantly critiquing the differences.

Others pointed out the difficulty of attracting graduate students to work with, a professional highlight for many scholars. Jose (Argentina to the United States) noted the problem:

> If you're an African American student, very likely, you gravitate to an African American faculty member. Or if you are Latina, or if you are Asian. If you are queer, as a student, likely, you might find some kind of empathy or connection. [...] Especially in a country that is so heavily invested in this kind of everyday identity politics. But I don't have that.

This interpretation was also reinforced by Juha (South Korea to the United States), who is teaching in a graduate program but feeling quite marginalized by the students:

> I see that my students cannot easily connect with me because I look different. When I was in the Midwest some students never saw any single Asian person before. And suddenly you see a professor who's Asian. That's when I feel that I have to break the distance between my students and me. [...] and this is probably truer at this HBCU [Historically Black Colleges and Universities] because 95 percent of my students are Black and they wonder, "Why is she here if she's not Black?" Because even the majority of the faculty members and administrators are Black. [...] I never felt so outside. [...] But you know, that when you are being categorized, you know, you get more conscious about that. When you know that you are the minority and you feel the pressure, the stress. Just being reminded that you are the minority can put the stress on you without realizing that it is a source of stress on you.

HyeJin (South Korea to the United States), too, perceived her intersectional identity as both a woman and an Asian immigrant as an obstacle to attracting strong graduate students. In attempting to explain why she doesn't have Ph.D. advisees, she said, "I know that many Ph.D. students, in general, prefer White male senior faculty. That's their highest priority."

Racism and Discrimination

George (Romania to the United States), quoted above, was not the only interviewee who interpreted racist undercurrent in his inability to be completely integrated into the host environment. Several of the narratives revealed not only processes of consistent othering but also some incidences of discrimination. While most of the participants were very reluctant to suggest that they encountered any racist or discriminatory attitudes toward them, the few who expressed that they had such experiences were very outspoken about it. It is particularly interesting to note that the vast majority of discriminatory narratives were relayed by women and in doing so evoked cases of intersectional themes. This is not surprising, given the accumulated scholarship on gender inequality in academia, including in salary and paths for promotion, student evaluation, stereotypes related to specific disciplines, and the like.[5] More specifically, research has demonstrated that student evaluations for women more generally, and women of color more specifically, are systematically lower than for White men.[6]

The lived experiences of participants in this study who are women of color contribute to this conclusion. Iracema (Brazil to Portugal), for example, explained prejudice against Brazilians: "It was really hard. Even with the students. I also saw their faces, and how surprised they were because I was Brazilian. If I say two words, everybody knows that I'm Brazilian. [...] I think in every country that had their colonies all the immigrants of ex-colonies are seen as [lower class]. [...] I had to work two times harder to prove myself."

Mona (Kuwait to the United States) had a particularly hard adjustment, and at the time of the interview was still struggling with rejections from positions she desired, and torn between challenges back home in a traditional environment and the new ones she encountered in the United States:

> Some people have suggested that search committees project their fears onto candidates, whether by detecting accents or in other ways. But then living in the Arab world was so traditional, it was suffocating at times. [...] I told my family, "I just can't do this." And they said, "Well. This was the only option you had. They didn't pick you to go work in other environments that you wanted. Right?" These kinds of

moments would sting because you could never tell—is it that, really, my work is not good enough and I need to do more to be accepted as a serious scholar? Or is it really that people look at your name and they look like, you know, "Can this person speak English?"

Violeta (Chile to the United States) discussed the potentially explosive relationships she has with graduate students over cultural differences and prejudice against female professors of color, raising the potential of intersectional discrimination:

> With the cultural climate—I certainly find myself being much more careful in terms of the words I use, and how I approach topics. I do feel like they do things to me that they would never do to [a White male professor] or to my friend [a White female professor]. I mean, you know, some of the emails I get—[. . .] I feel like they would not have done this to different racialized or even gendered people. [. . .] I gave a campus-wide lecture last year, and the first two questions were really hostile. And that's when a couple of my friends said, "Wow! Is that the kind of stuff you've been telling us about for the last twenty years?" I'm like, "Yeah. People feel like they can challenge a person of color, even of very little color, like me, in a way that they do not do to somebody like you." Me talking to my friends here, yeah. It was an eye-opener to them. [. . .] I have to really work hard to establish authority and to establish a respectful classroom. [. . .] I will treat you [students] respectfully, but just because you can tell immediately that I'm a Latina woman because of my accent, my name, and the way I look, that doesn't mean you can be disrespectful.

Violeta was not the only immigrant woman who experienced such treatment from students. Another story came from Eva (Brazil to Sweden): "It's very subtle. [. . .] If it's a Swedish class, I always have to assert myself. And then I feel there is less trust. And then, sometimes, the students say things and do things that they wouldn't do if it was a male Swedish professor. So that's just not only being Swedish but being a woman."

Ikechukwu (Nigeria to the United States), the only man discussed in this context, softened the argument by framing it as ignorance rather than discrimination: "I wouldn't call it discrimination. I would say that sometimes there is a lack of knowledge about Africa. And I did notice that at [a prestigious university] some of the teachers are surprised that they had no clue. I was studying advertising and I remember one teacher asking me why I was doing advertising—'Is there advertising in Nigeria?'—and I was shocked by that. I said, 'Yes.'"

Another related issue raised up by several academic immigrants to the United States was a tendency to generalize by grouping immigrants into stereotypical homogenous categories that ignored their backgrounds and identities. Wael (Jordan to the United States), a Christian Arab, said, "That's the assumption [that I am Muslim]. If you're an Arab, there's an assumption that you're Muslim. One of the many things that people don't know about the Middle East is that there are lots of minorities throughout the Middle East. I think the media don't cover it well. I think some people don't say it to your face, but they have that assumption and they make their own conclusion without talking about it."

Following a very long discussion of discrimination and marginalization throughout her academic career over both gender as well as race, Violeta (Chile to the United States), whom we met above, concluded, "A lot of people who immigrate here say, 'Well, you know, I thought of myself as a Chilean, or an Argentinian, or Colombian. But then I got to the United States and people started calling me a Mexican, and I'm not a Mexican. I'll be a Latina. So that's the point that people kind of transition from being whatever their nation's specificity into the general Latina category here, is in—because they're reacting negatively to being categorized as Mexican."

Imposing a nonrelevant generalization that carries potentially discriminatory overtones was also the experience of Hadas, from a very different background (Israel to the United States):

> For Israelis that are secular, coming to the U.S. and people think of you as Jewish-American, which is a completely different experience. [...] So I'm the associate chair and the chair happens to be Jewish, and apparently somebody said to somebody else, "Oh, the Jews are taking over the department." So obviously being Jewish also makes a difference, and when the campus is progressive, being Israeli is very difficult too [because of the Palestinian-Israeli conflict]. [...] For

example, I had a colleague who said to me once, "All you care about is money." I don't think she would have said it if I weren't Jewish. It was completely not related to anything in the real world. Not to my salary, really, to nothing. So I am sure there are a lot of anti-Israeli things said about me behind my back. Not to my face.

The side comment that Hadas made about difficulties being an Israeli in a progressive environment was clearly the experience of Maya (Israel to the United Kingdom), who described how torn she is about the criticism of Israel to the point that she, too, like Hadas (and often, like myself, too), tries to avoid discussions of politics.

> I feel very uncomfortable. And there are occasions, like around war especially, when it also becomes very visible because everybody's going to protests. And I'm always slightly ambivalent. I would have gone to the protest on the one hand; if I were in Israel, I would be the first one to the march. But I think it's just become so indiscriminately in terms of just a very broad brush for anti-Israel in every single respect that I feel hesitant to identify with. [. . .] It's complicated. The British have this tendency where they detect that your accent is not British—they are very curious to know where you're from. But they don't know how exactly to ask it. But anyway, sooner or later in the conversation, they will ask something: "Oh, and where are you from?" And I'm just thinking, "Well, I've been here for twenty years. Why does it matter?" But then I say, "I'm originally from Israel." And because Israel is also such an explosive thing, and I never know what their politics is, it makes it just really murky. And I find it always very surprising, even though also, London is so international. It's a mix of accents. Like, something that almost shouldn't have been an issue because, to start with, everybody always speaks with different accents. It still is something. [. . .] There is something about you being implicitly marked as a stranger.

Both Hadas and Maya's interviews took place two years before the October 7, 2023, Hamas massacre in Israel and the resulting ferocious war between Israel and Hamas lit the Middle East on fire; and yet, in many ways, they cited what would become significantly more extreme later on. Maya went on to describe her personal strategies for dealing with the internal identity conflicts she found herself engaged in, and continued to explain:

> I'm following Goffman's advice on backstage and front stage. And I really separate it. To be honest, I'm almost bracketing it out. [...] It's things like even... I'm preparing now an important lecture for my promotion. And I was thinking, "What do I want to say?" And I wanted to have slightly a biographical element to think about my academic trajectory and the like. And I was thinking about it and I'm thinking, "I don't, you know, it's a public event. I don't know if I want even to identify..." You know, I'm not gonna go on stage and say, "I'm an Israeli." But for instance, I did want to speak about my upbringing in the kibbutz as an important context for a lot of my thinking, especially about, you know, socialist imagination and the collective—and it's very central to me that has always been in all my work, thinking about collective structures and their absence. So, in any other context, I would have, of course, used it. [...] But this is just a tiny example of how, because I've also become so used to really blocking this aspect of my identity in my work and professional life, it's almost, you know, actually really, in some ways, sad. And in some ways, you're thinking, "It's such an important part of my identity." That's also, by the way, one of the reasons that I've barely done any research that involves Israel, although I would have loved to, and on many occasions throughout the years, some things interested me. And I wrote one piece about the international coverage of the Gaza war [in 2014]—just because the war offended me so much. And even on this, I received a lot of very problematic responses, you know. And it just almost proved that I shouldn't do it again. I should leave this untouched; I don't know.

Maya's painful narrative of identity struggles was provided in some detail because it highlights how the tendency to impose on one's origin a load of responsibility for the politics and cultures of the entire nation enforces a major loss of one's core self-image to be able to avoid unnecessary conflicts and negative relationships. Hiding central parts of one's identity is a heavy price that many academic immigrants have had to pay to protect themselves from harsh sentiments that may be completely not their own. The Israel-Hamas war that broke out in 2023 has become an excellent example of this struggle as former Israelis on campuses around the Western world have been ostracized, blamed, and harassed for the actions of their home country (that they left!).

Several other scholars interviewed addressed what they perceived as the patriarchal elitism and multiple forms of discrimination that they found in the academic world. Some testimonies of how gender and ethnicity intersect to shape their academic immigrant experiences have already been shared in previous pages. Here I share some of the more detailed and outspoken examples of interviewees who reflected on the issues quite boldly. They echo scholarship on hegemonic White masculinity in multiple ways.[7] Lynn (the United States to Europe), a White woman in a dominant White environment, reflected on this from a more removed posture:

> They are trying to be gender equal—that's not really there yet. I think many spaces around the world are not there yet, and there have clearly been many points where I've had to find my voice as a female, and that's made it feel even more uncomfortable because I'm also foreign, so, this is like, "How much can I push this?" There's like a double dose of challenge, I think. And I can imagine it's even further the more angles of diversity you experience.

Indeed, when ethnicity or race gets in the mix, the web of challenges becomes significantly more complicated. For example, Meena (India to the United States) shared,

> That's the constant experience, you know, of sexism [. . .] how I was infantilized. So for instance, there's this grant that faculty apply for, and if you're granted the grant, you're given the money up front. But I was told, "I'm sorry, you need to spend the money first and then we'll give it to you," and I said, "Why? I mean, every other faculty member you give it . . ." "Oh, we think you might lose it." I'm like, "Do you think I'm going to carry the money in my pocket and it's going to fall out of my pocket? What is the meaning of this treatment?" So it was just, you know, always there was this double standard. [. . .] That was a strange and bewildering experience, to come to this country and experience this.

Daniela (Colombia to the United States) related two specific incidences to illustrate the depth of the discrimination she is feeling, in the following long, painful, and very insightful monologue:

> I encounter it [demeaning exchanges with men] a lot. Let me give you some examples. A year ago—I was around here in a restaurant. I was eating on my own. And two colleagues from the university came. They're White husband and wife. And they came to the restaurant and then, you know, they were kind of startled that I was there. And like, "Oh, oh, what are you doing here?" And then he said, "What are you doing here? Do you work here washing dishes?" [. . .] I didn't say anything at that moment. But [later] I made a big deal out of it with her, because I trust her. And so, I talked to her and said, "Okay, can you please tell your husband to not make that kind of joke around me because—I mean, would he say that if I was a White male sitting there? 'Course not." [. . .] I'm a Latina, so, all the images of Latina maids are popping into his head, and that's what he is bringing to the table. Even though he has interacted with me. He came to my job talk and he knows that I have not an inch of the experience of being a maid. [. . .]
>
> Once—one of the worst experiences, and I don't even know how to articulate or codify this, in one of my own professional evaluation meetings at the university with the chair, when I was still untenured, [. . .] he was questioning some of my publication venues. So, I was explaining—because they're Latin American. And at one point, one of the most prestigious journals in Colombia had published an article in that, and he was comparing it—which I have no idea, like, with what criteria—to a very obscure regional journal in, like, the southern states, or something. And that made me cry. [. . .] My dignity was crushed. [. . .] To think that this guy could compare, you know, a prestigious—and it didn't matter how much I argued and gave him evidence of the prestige of the journal. No, he just had it in his mind that, because it came from there, you know, it had to be at the same stature as this other journal.
>
> I think, in my experience, the kind of othering and marginalization that I felt is more on people putting down and insulting Latin American academia and Latin American efforts and Latin American ideas and Latin American theories and Latin American methodologies and Latin American . . . that hurt me to a point where the joke about, you know, dishwashing doesn't.

The intersection of nationality and gender, being an Israeli and a strong woman, in a particular national context, provided Dana (Israel to the United States) with particular experiences and points of view:

> Well, being an outspoken, powerful female Israeli, I was often misunderstood. But all this, you know, to be honest, can I curse? It's the f-cking chauvinism everywhere, right? [...] But I will tell you that the otherness has to do with definitely the intercultural thing. Being Israeli, to begin with, is a lot more direct. And you know, it took me a long while to understand and kind of massage my presentation. I'll give you an example. You have a meeting and somebody has an idea in the United States and everybody hates the idea. What do they say? They go, "Great idea! But how about..." and then they say the opposite of your idea. And the meeting lasts for three hours until you kind of understand they didn't like your idea at all. Yeah, I mean, I would just go, "Oh, that's a terrible idea. I'm moving on." [...] The very direct—and, you know, I would say that New Yorkers kind of understood me always. Like, people from New York and LA. But I was in the South, so, that was a big thing. People would respond to me that, you know, I think I'm so nice, and they're like, "Oh, you're so aggressive."

In reflecting on the interviews I conducted with many of my female interviewees, women who left their home country, family, and friends and embarked courageously on a journey that required independence, resilience, talent, and determination were in many ways nonconventional in their traditional societies, perhaps even rebels of sorts. Meena (India to the United States), Daniela (Colombia to the United States), Rumia (India to the United States), Enrichetta (Italy to the United States), Violeta (Chile to the United States), Dana (Israel to the United States), HyeJin (South Korea to the United States)—to name just a few—all shared narratives of breaking boundaries, not only geographical but also cultural and social associated with ethnicity and gender expectations and stereotypes.

Violeta (Chile to the United States), whose voice we heard several times, summarized the intersectionality issue, but gave it a very positive spin at the end:

> The conflation of both the gender and the ethnicity—'cause if you were just a woman, we know what those issues are. If you're just a

Latino—a person from Chile, maybe it would have been different. [...] It definitely is intersectional, because I can't tease out, "Oh, that was because I'm a woman. This is because, you know, I'm Latina." It just functions as an additive kind of process. Most of them are engaging in implicit racism, not explicit racism. But it just kind of takes off two of these implicit categories that allow them to say more and to treat me with less authority and respect. [...]

But you know, we are the winners. We are the winners of second-wave feminism. We're feminists, we are in a Research 1 university, and we're full professors. I mean, don't lose sight of that. I don't lose sight of what that means, of the role model that that means for my students and my junior faculty. And of the thorn in the side that I need for mainstream kind of professors when I say, "Well, why don't we think about diversity in this committee?" And if I weren't there, nobody would bring that up, right?

Several other social groups in higher education—including racially minoritized faculty and faculty with disabilities—have similar experiences of alienation within the academy. However, the nature of the alienation is often compounded for academic immigrants, as many have minoritized, racialized, and/or cultural identities and, additionally, face the challenges of being foreign to this country. Gender inequalities just add another layer of complexity to the mix.

Adjustment

Yet, despite it all, my interviewees held on, learned to manage the challenges, and developed strategies of adaptation and acceptance that this sense of otherness is here to stay. Dick (the United States to Europe to Singapore) described it to me in these terms: "I've lived abroad for more than thirty years. And still, when I come back to the States—there's this ambient just sort of, I get it. I understand what's happening. I understand the little things I should say and do in a way that I don't understand in other places. That I'll never, you know, I get by really well in other places, but I can't really always read the situation at the level that I can read it here."

Some of the participants filled the need for a stronger sense of belonging by socializing with their fellow compatriots and maintaining a close network of cultural ties. Others resisted that tendency on purpose, as did Yee (Hong Kong to the United Kingdom), who did not anticipate the difficulties she would encounter and also made a conscious decision to do her best to adapt to the local culture and stay away from only socializing with people with a similar background like hers:

> Even though we were a British colony when I was growing up, maybe a lot of people didn't really have that much ties to Britain. But at the same time, I think because I was always educated in English and so, I felt that I was able to live here in a way, kind of quite successfully. But at the same time, I came to this very small city in Northern England. So, there was, in fact, quite a lot of racism. So, whether it's directly against me or not, I was kind of aware of that. You know, people making kind of, like comments, or just sort of having a joke about race and stuff like this. So I always kind of picked that up. But I kind of never really wanted that to be against me. I'd think to myself, "I'm just going to do what I want to do. And I'm not going to let this fear that people will discriminate against me to work against what I want to do." [...] I am interested in other people and I didn't seek out other Chinese people as much. So actually, I had that kind of idea that I don't want to be just with other people from the same background.

Similarly, Rachel (Canada to the United Kingdom) related her decision to stay away from other Canadians:

> There were a few other Canadians at my institution at the time and their solution was to just stay together. They had lunch together, they went to the pub together, they had family dinners together. And they included me, and they did nothing but complain about the United Kingdom. And I think after—probably it wasn't more than a year before I said, "I'm sorry, I'm not doing this." And so, I stopped. And so, then, I was completely isolated for quite a while. [...] Because I didn't think that I should be complaining about a place I had chosen to live. I thought, "I either have to get to like this country in some sense or leave." And so, I said to myself, "If you're going to stay here, you bloody well better figure out how to live in this country." And so, I did.

However, as the conversation unfolded, she admitted that she continued to feel as an outsider after thirty years:

> I know that I've always thought that it [feeling as a foreigner] was a very awkward kind of thing that's never, ever resolved itself. And in a way, I think that awkwardness is productive. I think it has also, over the thirty years or so, been negatively unhelpful. I wish I'd assimilated somehow more, in some ways. So, I think it's just something that installed itself in my head. [...] But if you ask my colleagues, they would say I've assimilated 100 percent. So, this story I'm telling you is my perception; it's not everyone's perception.

Accepting—and even rationalizing—why they are not, could not be, and perhaps even should not be—fully integrated was strongly tied to my participants' choice to dwell on the positive aspects of their "otherness" and the unique values they bring to academia. This is the focus of the next chapter.

5

The Benefits

What Are These Academics Uniquely Contributing?

"The Perspective That Others Can't See"

As we have demonstrated, first, the double life that characterizes the majority of my interviewees comes with a host of challenges—but also offers tremendous value and a variety of benefits to immigrant academics, their departments, institutions of higher education, and the academic world at large. Second, the outsider-insider position that the academic immigrants occupy allows them to develop a unique perspective on the "taken for granted" social phenomenon, a potential to disrupt existing routines and expectations and to serve as a catalyst for the creation of new knowledge and ways of seeing. Third, their displacement brings with it a heightened awareness of a need to critically rethink existing paradigms and knowledge structures, as strangeness and intellectuality seem to be strongly connected.[1]

These dualities invoke the well-known concept of "the stranger" introduced by Georg Simmel already over a century ago.[2] It is worth a reminder of the richness of this concept via two direct quotes from Simmel that explain as well as demonstrate the relevancy of this concept to our inquiry here: "The stranger is thus being discussed here, not in the sense often touched upon in the past, as the wanderer who comes today and goes tomorrow, but rather as the person who comes today and stays tomorrow. He is, so to speak, the potential wanderer; although he has not moved on, he has not quite overcome the freedom of coming and going" (402).

These characteristics seem to be most appropriate for the vast majority of the participants in the study who moved to and settled in another country. The few who did eventually move again usually stayed for a significant number of years in each academic institution before moving on.

Later in Simmel's seminal article, he adds, "The principal point of interest has been that a person may be a member of a group in a spatial sense but still not be a member of the group in a social sense; that a person may be in the group but not of it" (403).

Occupying such a position in a group is both familiar and foreign and allows the "stranger" more freedom from habits and norms, and thus, according to Simmel, to be perceived as more objective, and more likely to be valued as someone with whom one can confide. Furthermore, several interpreters of Simmel remind us that many notable contributions to humanity were made by transnational "strangers" who lived in exile from their homeland, including great intellectuals of the twentieth century, such as Theodore Adorno, Hannah Arendt, Zygmunt Bauman, Jacques Derrida, Albert Einstein, Stuart Hall, Herbert Marcuse, and Edward Said—to name just a few. So, while the "stranger" is often viewed somewhat with suspicion by the inside group and as a result encounters a host of challenges, as discussed in the previous chapter, she or he also has unique advantages that were very well recognized by the participants in the study and expressed in their interviews.[3]

The benefits that the participants in the study talked about referred to the three pillars of the academic world: scholarship, teaching, and service. While most of the emphasis was put on original scholarship, significant parts of their accounts also focused on teaching. The leadership part of service played a minor role, perhaps because only a few of the interviewees occupied positions as academic administrators at the time of the interview.

Scholarly Contributions

As they reflected on their academic interests and passions, many interviewees were found to be very much aware of what their unique position offered them and spoke about it in their interviews.

Immigrant Sensibility

An immigrant's experience and sensibility impacted what they were passionate about studying as scholars. Anna (Cyprus/Greece to the United Kingdom) explained her scholarly interests in this way:

> So, I guess my family's history of migration [...] it's like there's no coincidence at all that I'm interested in studying migration. [...] I think I can see things that have to do with difference. That has to do with my own experience. And of course, you know, that links to both teaching and research. [...] So I think there are a lot of qualities of being an outsider. [...] This is a political project for me. [...] I'm absolutely confident that, you know, there is a reason I do this work: I think the fact that it is so close to my heart and with everything that has to do with me.

George (Romania to the United States) stated it very concisely: "I was interested in research on the impact of moving from one culture to another. On the issues related to cultural shock." So did Juan (Mexico to the United States): "I would say I'm interested in transnational issues. And so, my work deals with things that move across borders. Either media or people," referring to the flow of bodies, ideas, cultural products and the like that take place across national borders.

The sense of "otherness" that is a dominant part of the lived experience of immigration led many of the interviewees (all of whom, as noted, were in the social sciences) to study diversity, equity, and inclusion issues (DEI). The following narrative quotes illustrate this theme.

Mayur (India to the United States) explained his sensitivity to DEI issues: "So issues like diversity and inclusion are more personal to me. That is not something that I just learned because somebody said we should care about this. You know, it's something that I had to kind of work through."

Jae-Joon (South Korea to the United States) also attributed his focus on disparities to his ability to bring a unique perspective as an immigrant:

> I study discrimination and inequality in many aspects. One of my questions still comes from my story. Being an immigrant, being an Asian, being a Korean, being a first-generation immigrant, and being a man is very different than any other immigration story. I think this motivates me, about the inequality side of it. I'm really concerned about multicultural identity issues, and economic disparity. [...] That's the kind of work that I am working on. The fact that I'm a very outsider, an immigrant, actually allows me to see this kind of unique environment. That stuff, a perspective that not anyone can see.

Meena (India to the United States) also reflected, "My research has always been other-oriented because of the fact that I do not fit in, and I didn't feel a need to study myself."

Savitri (India to the United States) developed this theme further:

> The fact of migration and mobility; not only do I study them now, but I think being a diasporic intellectual has constantly shaped the questions I ask, the issues I deal with, and the kinds of interventions that I want to make. You know, I don't think immigration has just been about the fact of moving, but it has shaped my scholarly life in profound ways. [...] My mobility, my feminist beliefs, and my approach to academic work as a form of intervention for social justice are all connected. [...] Developing a global expansive approach to the study of migration is my scholarly preoccupation. And I think, in a way, there are parallel tracks with my own global moves.

Mina (India to the United States) went into more detail in relating her interest in racial dynamics conflated with her desire to understand her situation:

> Certainly, being an immigrant is what highly shaped my research in what I picked to do [...] because I got a clear sense of race after coming to the U.S. Until then, I never thought about race much. I thought a lot about gender. When I came to the U.S., I could see the racial dynamics, and so it was kind of important for me to understand,

"Where do I fit in the society" and, you know, "How do I learn about different people?" And I learned a lot about different groups from popular culture. And then I got afraid, like, I'm making these stereotypes about different groups in the U.S. through that. And I could see that. So, I wanted to connect with actual people, and so on. So, my work was very much shaped by that experience in the choice of what I studied.

The process of immigration—the uprooting and re-rooting—brings to the surface dormant sensibilities and catalyzes self-identity explorations. Such, for example, was shared by Mona (Kuwait to the United States), who chose to focus on her proud Arab identity and the tendency for a "me-search" approach to scholarship:

> My area of research is intercultural and international communication. [...] There are many reasons to be proud of being Arab and the social progress of the last few decades. But I thought, "Okay, I'm going to have to do something about this." So, I actually write projects where I see a compelling need. [...] I feel like my growing up between two vastly different world regions—my questions really are just trying to fill in all these different gaps. [...] You have to use the scientific method and rely on previous literature. But like, you know, "me-search" is one of the terms that I was taught to use. It's like the questions that come to you. It's almost like, you select the questions that make the most sense to you.

Studying One's Home Country

The most obvious and unique way participants brought something new to their disciplines was by advancing research projects that focus on their home country. Their advantage was clear over non-natives due to having mastery of their home language, understanding the intricacies of the culture and the social-political-historical context, and accessing networks of colleagues and fostering collaborations. Here are but a few of the many examples gathered in chatting with interviewees: A Chinese immigrant studying Chinese media. A Nigerian immigrant studying Nigerian social networks. An Italian immigrant studying Italian neofascist movements. A Colombian immigrant studying Latin American social movements. An Israeli immigrant studying media in conflict zones. An Indian immigrant studying Bollywood. An immigrant from Cameroon studying Black Diasporas.

Interviewees had no difficulty explaining their choices. Cosmas (Nigeria to the United States) explained as follows: "I have to look at my area from an African perspective. Yes, we have millions of papers about the United States, but I like to do something as it relates to Africa, the multidisciplinary issues surrounding the African Diaspora."

Smita (India to the United States) combined several personal threads in explaining her approach to her research that focuses on her home country:

> This outsiderness that I felt, you know, as a young woman, became fuel for me to do research. Why did I feel like an outsider? What was going on? And words like "patriarchy"—how that is wedded to ideas of nationhood, right? How sexuality and women's sexuality become a symbol or the emblem of the nation. All of these things started making sense to me. So, my roots, you know, the roots that I had . . . but also the feelings of alienation. [. . .] So, these crevices and spaces between one's political identity and one's native cultural identity became fodder for me to do my research. [. . .] So, 90 percent of my research is on India. And it will continue to be [so].

These projects in themselves have tremendous value in expanding social science disciplines, dismantling the U.S.-centric dominance of academia worldwide, and enriching our views and knowledge of the world outside our own "place."

Knowledge Brokers

Bringing something new to their scholarly communities went well beyond the selection of topics for study, as they were able to offer different perspectives and approaches, as Anne (Canada to the United Kingdom) explained:

> So, the thing was, I was the only person in my school [in the United Kingdom] who was doing feminist research. So, then, I did feel that my perspective was—maybe coming from Canada was a bit different from both America and the U.K. [. . .] I was already kind of a bit of an outsider

in the field because Americans didn't really do the British stuff, and the British didn't really do the American stuff. So, I felt like I was a bit of a bridge for some people. You know, bringing them together, those perspectives too. I kind of tried to make a virtue of that.

A unique perspective was offered by Evan (Belgium to Europe), who in many ways sees himself as an academic nomad, one who can easily move from one place to another and leverage this capacity for his choice of scholarship:

> I think I'm just lucky in the sense that I'm curious and, apparently, I have the ability to enter into other people's worlds. Which I think is a key research skill. And I've been lucky enough not to get locked into particular nation-states which does allow me to travel, but not in a physical, but in a mental, intellectual way. [...] The kind of work I do is not necessarily linked to particular regions. I'm interested in interesting case studies. [...] You know, the feeling when something really turns out to be fascinating, and where you know that you can tell a story about it, because you know that's what we do. We tell stories in academic ways. I am simply lucky that I can find stories all over the world.

Many of the interviewees leveraged their "otherness" as a source of pride and self-fulfillment and focused particularly on their ability to expand upon what they perceived to be the U.S.-centric, exceptionalist perspectives enacted by many American academics. Tamir (Israel to the United States) shared this perspective: "My otherness became a big part of how I was able to contribute to the conversation in the field because, you know, people were telling me, 'Oh, you're doing international research' and I was like, 'Nope, no. I'm doing other national.' It was destabilizing. [...] It allows me to step back and say, 'I, you know, have something to add to your perspective that's in your blind spot.'"

A central endeavor of interviewees' scholarship involves applying comparative approaches and perspectives in studies of aspects of the universal versus the particular in national settings. Eddy (Europe to Israel) developed the value of such research that breaks the boundaries of one's national research:

It's really deeply connected to my research. When I was in Europe, my research was squarely European. [...] The same in the U.S., same in the U.K. It's changing now. More and more people are aware that they're talking about their own nationality in a global world. And that's something experienced at a very personal level. So, I think the uniqueness of being an outsider is that you always compare. You're always aware of the singular character of any kind of national data you examine. You consider why it's happening this way. Is it because it is Israel? Or it's something global? And you realize that international patterns, global patterns, may be uniquely local patterns.

Similarly, Nadya (Bulgaria to the United States) was also looking for the difference between culturally specific findings, through a comparative lens, when she said,

I would be interested [in doing research in Bulgaria]. It's a different perspective. I've been thinking about it more recently because, in many disciplines, mine included, scholarship is very U.S.-centric. [...] It makes it more difficult to get a sense of what part of the research is culturally specific and what will translate to other places. So, I think about how something can be expanded to look at eastern Europe and Bulgaria.

In summary, these findings suggest that academic immigrants can serve as knowledge brokers bridging cultures and academic spaces.[4] This is very apparent if we view the academic world as a global enterprise. Here, migrant academics serve as stimulators and facilitators of many endeavors: they are authors and editors of international journals, and participants in conferences as well as exchange programs. In doing so they forge international collaborations and advance networks for colleagues and students, host visits by guest lecturers, draw international students, provide access to scholarship published in many languages, and expand their institutional sources of funding by tapping into international foundations.

These colleagues approach scholarship from diverse perspectives and theoretical groundings. They are also serving as intermediaries who are capable of looking both ways—inward to their roots in their home country and outward toward their host culture—and in doing so, they create and broker new knowledge, opportunities, and synergies.[5]

Personal Motivations

There are many incentives for academic immigrants to engage in this work, and through their engagement, they carve out a unique space of expertise for themselves. Doing so also provides them with opportunities to maintain connections to their homeland, as they can travel back and forth to visit colleagues, family, and friends, and maintain a strong sense of belonging.

Some also seem to feel that this enables them to ease their guilt feelings about leaving their original home in the first place and to cultivate a sense of giving back and helping out from afar. Such, for example, was the narrative provided by Demetrios (Greece to the United States):

> Part of the reason I went back [on a research project] was to see whether I could do things in Greece that would in some minor way make me feel at least that I was doing something to contribute back to Greece, and maybe addressing some issues that had to do with the economic crisis and its effects. [...] It was the first push toward thinking about how my work could be more focused on Greece, and how it might contribute to something positive on the other side of the Atlantic. It's great that it means that I have excuses to go back to Greece more often to see family and friends, but, you know, that wasn't the driver at the time.

Similarly, Violeta (Chile to the United States) explained, "It's my identity. I want to help my kin. I feel like I wouldn't be here if it weren't for my primary education. I am connected to Chile in all of those many ways. [...] I'm very engaged and trying to contribute. This is a desire to give back to the home country in my own career."

I strongly identified with the sense of commitment that these interviewees expressed. I have developed a reputation as the "girl who can't say no" to any request from Israel to review a research proposal, to judge a dissertation, to serve on a committee, to advise a student. Whatever the request, I felt the obligation to take it upon myself indiscriminately.

Teaching Contributions

In addition to its influence on research, the outsider perspective plays a very important role in the pedagogical practices of academic immigrants. Even beyond sharing their perspectives, viewed more broadly, they are contributing in a variety of ways to the higher education mission of cultivating critical thinkers, global citizens, and active participants in a strong democracy. Rumia (India to the United States) explained:

> My goal always has been to connect them to the larger world we live in rather than, you know, thinking the U.S. is the center of the world. So that has always been my push in whatever I'm teaching. [...] Whatever it is, just to sort of widen it up and say, "You know, there are many ways and orientations and ways of looking at the world and understanding reality." [...] I think the immigration experience sort of relativizes your sense of place in the world.

Students crave connections with faculty members that highlight and value diversity, recognize them as important members of the institution, and demonstrate respect and interest toward their home culture and language and its contributions to society.[6] As noted by Mina (India to the United States), "I bring international aspects of the world into every class that I teach. Because I feel like, you cannot be U.S.-centric when you're teaching. That's doing a disservice to my students. [...] In fact, one of my grad students said, 'This is the first time I am seeing myself in a syllabus. I'm seeing myself.' For me, that was the best compliment."

Pedagogical Strategies

Several interviewees talked about the way they turned their otherness into an explicit pedagogical strategy. Smita (India to the United States) explained how cultivating a critical approach to her teaching is born from her comparative approach to the two cultures she lived in:

> My bicultural background completely influences my teaching, in that I come from a very, very poor country. When I left, India was just called a third-world country. [...] And so, coming from that to a very

prosperous country, and the politics of that prosperity or the politics of the poverty, and systems of hierarchy in India and in the U.S., there is a comparative perspective. [...] Because you come from two different cultures, you cannot escape critique.

Alisha (India to the United States) refers to her various cultural experiences as an asset to her teaching as well:

This cross-cultural experience has helped me a lot in terms of understanding the content of my teaching. So I give them these examples, and sometimes I show them the case studies. Because I feel the Americans are really clueless about what is happening in the world around them. [...] Sometimes they are totally amazed when I tell them that this is what happens in England, or this is what happens in the East, in India. So international exposure has brought in a lot of cultural orientations to add to my knowledge and to impart that knowledge in teaching.

Interviewees with other backgrounds expressed similar sentiments. Gaus (Pakistan to the United States), who teaches journalism, brings an applied perspective from his background and networks to the classroom:

I bring examples from Pakistan, and from other countries that I know of. But I mainly discuss the experiences of my friends or invite friends to classrooms to share their experiences with the students to see how students are pressured in case they go out and report from a country other than the U.S. How are they going to deal with the situation? And what were the principles of news reporting applied in the U.S. and other countries, and what are the differences? So, I try to bring those experiences to the classroom.

Coming from a very different background, Fintan (Ireland to New Zealand) used his background as a resource for teaching: "I would routinely draw on Irish examples and personal examples in class. And I would routinely draw on students' familiarity with Irish stereotypes, and get certain pleasure out of playing with the stereotypes to make some theoretical point."

Ikechukwu (Nigeria to the United States) extends the use of what he refers to as African knowledge in textbook writing to facilitate teaching:

> I give a lot of African examples. For example, I wrote the first textbook that I'm using today in my class when I teach the introduction to the topic. [...] In that book, one of the things that I made sure of, because other textbooks in this area prior to that time that I've looked at were basically all focused on American examples. So, I decided to do an international version. And one of the key things I made sure of is that the cases in there would deal with different kinds of issues and different countries. It wasn't going to be focused on the U.S. [...] I try and make sure that African issues are represented.

Tanzoui (Cameroon to the United States), another African participant, was strongly motivated by the mission of employing pedagogy for doing good and leveraged his African connections and travels as assets that allowed him to work toward this goal with his American students. He explained, "It makes me happy. That's why I keep telling you that I travel a lot. I help Ph.D. students in universities in Africa, both electronically and in person. Why? Because I believe in the mission of changing the mind. Remember, I want to decolonize their minds, too. Also, to have some sense of self-worth."

Claire (Canada to the United States) provided a specific example of the value of offering concrete comparative case studies to expand her students' horizons and teach them to question the taken for granted in their country:

> When we talk about the First Amendment and freedom of the press—that is so different between our two countries. I'm able to bring this idea that, you know, this isn't how it is everywhere. Right? Hate speech isn't legal in a lot of other places. And so we're able to have a conversation about that. And I'm coming to it from this outside perspective. [...] It allows them to say, "Oh yeah, these are the rules that are here, and they certainly matter the most because it's the rules we're operating under, but other countries don't necessarily follow these rules the same way."

Common pedagogical practices employed by many of my interviewees include sharing examples from other cultures, discussing current events from different cultural perspectives, sharing one's own experiences, and inviting guest lectures by international colleagues. Xiaolan (China to the United States) shared, "Most of the students are White, from very rich families. So, in this case, when I share my experience in China or my culture in China or, for example, I show them some TV programs in China, students are very, very excited. And you know, in my teaching evaluations some students would say, 'I like when you teach and bring some Chinese culture to the classroom.'"

Similarly, Cosmos (Nigeria to the United States) prides himself on being a very international person. Here he highlights its advantages in comparison to American colleagues:

> Because the American colleague, for instance, can give examples with the White House. Congress. That's about it. But me? For students, I not only tell them about the White House. I go to the White House in Kenya. The White House in Nigeria. The White House in Bangladesh. [. . .] I pull my experiences from all over the world, and students are like "Okay, this is what we want. What we need." So I think international people have that advantage.

Elena (Russia to the United States) also discussed the use of examples from Russia in-class sessions and added a clarifying comment: "Some subtle understandings of things that I developed because of being an outsider: I have a lot of examples that are relevant to my students for their culture, like things that are happening now that they can connect with. But maybe because I'm an outsider, I can see them a little differently."

Wael (Jordan to the United States) expressed his eagerness to find ways to educate his students about the Arab world. He related,

> So, we were doing this class on socio-materiality, and we wrote five different case studies for the students. And one of them was about the Arab Spring. It's part of something I was thinking about from my life in Jordan, and it was always something that I wanted to write about. And I ended up writing about it in a case study for teaching a class. And I think that part of me wanted to talk about

this background, and part of me wanted to teach the students about the Middle East. I got them to read about everything, starting with the Ottoman Empire and going up to 2011. So they learned a lot of things that I think they otherwise wouldn't know about the region. [...] So, yes, I did bring some of my cultural background into it.

A somewhat unique example of how her background impacted her teaching was offered by Paula (Germany to the United Kingdom). Rather than referring to the content of her teaching, she focused on cultivating structure and logical thinking in her students' work, attributing her approach to her German education:

> Sometimes I think that where I differ from many other colleagues is in approaching students' writing. When I see my comments when I mark essays, and I compare them to colleagues, I can see that I put a lot more emphasis on logic and structure. [...] I can really see that my British colleagues hardly ever comment on this. And sometimes, you know, when I'm moderating or I'm second marking, I'm kind of having these discussions where I go, "But it's so badly written and it barely makes sense," and they say, "Yeah, but I can see what the student wants to say." And I say, "Sorry, you know, this is just—it's not there in writing." So, this is where, sometimes, we have differences.

Finally, several of the interviewees shared that they try to enrich their students' lives by sharing their cultural traditions with them. For example, Xiaolan (China to the United States) shared: "We have celebrations or parties for our Chinese students from time to time, during the Chinese New Year festival, and other traditional Chinese festivals." For Satya (India to Sweden), sharing with students was also a way of affirming her identity, something she perceived as having some risks involved for her: "Today, I do everything—and sometimes it hurts me in academia—I do everything to assert my Hindu identity. On purpose. I didn't do that for many years. [...] I will take Indian festivals, like, everybody sends Christmas wishes, I will send wishes on Indian festivals to people and explain what it is. I will bring sweets for that day. The biggest thing I do is wear traditional Indian clothes. [...] As a scholar, that was my contribution."

Outing Oneself and Relating to Students

"Outing" oneself as an outsider seems to be a very common strategy to gain authority, interest, and legitimacy to bring their world into the classroom. Interviewees noted they did so often, and with a different voice and accent, as well. Enrichetta (Italy to the United States) described the process that she found worked best for her:

> So, I opened the conversation and said, "So, you know, am I White for you? Who am I for you? Am I White? Do you see a White middle-class, middle-aged woman? What do you see?" And this kid said, "Well, when you came in the first time, we thought you were White. But then you opened your mouth and we realize, no, she is not White [Laughs]."
>
> So, I think, especially in those years, you know, it took me some courage to open up these discussions in the classroom. I am always trying to point out my perspective, the fact that I can come from another part of the world and I try to give to my classroom a different perspective. [. . .] It's only in the last two or three years that I really started to be bolder about race, about my placement, my location, and not be afraid of saying stupid things or maybe using terms that are not accurate. And, indeed, I start by saying, you know, "I was not brought up here. I don't really know. I should know more. Teach me. I need to know from you what is this about. What is happening here?" So, we have had some fantastic conversations.

Positioning oneself as an outsider turned out to be a pedagogical strategy that facilitated mutual learning about the place of culture, race, and otherness—directly and openly. I, too, learned the value of employing such open positioning from doing research with young children in the United States. It gave me the license to ask them questions that would have possibly been disingenuous to them if I were a local adult, questions such as "I am new in this city; can you explain to me what is advertising on TV?" were welcomed with eagerness, as if they thought they could "teach me" something they felt they knew well, while I, as this foreign grown-up woman with a strange accent, did not know.

Another important strategy was to bring examples from other cultures that resonate strongly with the students' lived experiences.

Daniela (Colombia to the United States) presented such an illustration:

> Many of my students come from communities that are immersed in armed conflict, but we don't call it that. We call it gun violence, you know, for example, inner cities. So really, what you have is a group of unarmed civilians surrounded by men with guns. And so, it's exactly the same as my fieldwork in Colombia. [...] But they never thought about how media and communication can help these unarmed civilians resist and buffer the impact of armed conflict on their everyday lives. And when I teach about my own fieldwork and what others have done in African societies, Northern Ireland, Rwanda, and places like Mexico, it's like things click in their minds. [...] So it is very rewarding.

Bringing a very different personal history, Yerim (South Korea to the United States) also felt that her immigration background resonated with other students, regardless of their origin:

> I do emphasize that I can relate to a lot of you, who are either traveling abroad or who are currently studying abroad. Sometimes students would come up to me and want to talk about those things, you know. "Oh, I had a similar experience. My parents were the same way." Whatever example I used, they would just come up to me, and I could really sense that they wanted that sense of connection with their instructor. So that was really valuable. They don't have to be Asians, and they don't have to be Koreans.

The value of such sharing by faculty members with their students of second (or one and a half) generations of immigrant families has been documented in other research as well, as cited above.[7]

Occasionally interviewees explained their use of self-deprecating humor regarding their immigrant status to deal with potential discomfort in the classroom; for example, making fun of their own accent and language imperfections to unpack students' potential hostility and frustration. Jozef (Belgium to the United States) described this approach: "I catch myself worrying about not being aware of all the sensitivities of college students in the U.S. because it's such a big deal. And then I joke, like 'Hey, I'm an immigrant, I'm from Europe, I may be saying something you don't like to hear.' And so far, they seem to think that's funny."

This strategy also allowed for some self-deprecating humor about linguistic mistakes, being caught short of words, or misunderstanding a question. Speaking from my own experience, I often found myself stopping in the middle of a sentence and saying to my student, "How do you say in English this or that? I don't know the term for it." Or, I would say—there is a wonderful expression in Hebrew that says this or that—"Do you have something like this in English as well?" My experience has taught me that being very honest and humble about the shortcomings of not being a native speaker is mostly appreciated and invokes a lot of goodwill and helpfulness.

Lillian (Canada to the United States) also shared a similar strategy of reminding her students that she is Canadian:

> I very often refer to being Canadian [...] as a way of saying, "We're going to talk about maybe some challenging things, and I want to be with you on the outside looking in at these things, and so I'm going take my Canadian perspective." [...] Often it kind of lets me get away with making bad jokes. I just, you know, I use it as a device to also be self-deprecating. I really do use it as an identity marker very often. I often will say, you know, "The way I approach this is really from being Canadian. And it informs how I approach this intellectual problem or this academic issue. And so on. And maybe it can bring something to the table because I know you guys know the American way, but here's another way of looking at it."

In summary, sharing case studies from around the world, examples from other cultures, discussions of current events, and one's own experiences are all common pedagogical practices shared by many of my interviewees. Furthermore, many interviewees understand that despite the challenges and costs involved with being an outsider in the classroom, their presence is also a source of immense value for students and their institution's educational mission. This realization is seen clearly in the observation shared by Leo Yin (China): "I realized that my advantage is in my own historical background. My own cultural background, including my own academic background. So, I began to realize my strengths. I realized that instead of trying to abandon those, I tried to build on those past experiences."

Furthermore, many of my interviewees understand that being an outsider in the classroom is a resource of immense value for students. Their social positioning as an "other," as one often marginalized in academic circles (not to mention in the societies within which they chose to live), gives them a critical edge.

Leadership and Interaction Contributions

Interviewees acknowledged the fact that management and leadership roles at institutions of higher education in each country reflect that culture and so may differ from one culture to another. A few of the participants working in such roles related to what they bring that is unique to their positions. Jose (Argentina to the United States) provided his analysis of the cultural differences that he encountered to exemplify the more general issue:

> These jobs are designed for Americans in American society at an American university. So, you need to conform to the expectations of this job that are [...] culturally embedded in the way that Americans think about people in management or leadership positions. [...]
>
> I come from a country in which nobody expects leaders to be cheerleaders. That would sound, like, fake. You don't have to be inspirational, either. But here you have to be a little bit inspirational when you have a position of director or dean. You cannot just be a good manager. You need to show a certain sense of empathy and understanding. [...] You have to show that you care about personal well-being in a space that actually, clearly, demarcates separation between personal and professional. It is very different from where I come from. [...] Here you are expected to do it publicly, to make statements about events, to share your feelings about events publicly. You have to step into that role. [...] I check with colleagues who are in similar positions in other countries and they are not expected to do it in ways that are expected here.

The empirical part of this study was conducted at a time when American society was struggling with racial unrest and awakening following several horrendous killings of Black men by police and the emergence of a strong Black Lives Matter movement. At the time, there was a palpable expectation around campuses, from the ground up, for faculty and staff in many institutions of higher education in democratic states to express support and compassion. As a dean myself during these times, I witnessed the internal debates by higher administration of when and what is expected and by whom, and the risks of backlash from donors, politicians, and the public at large.

Since then, a few years have passed, and many university leaders across the country have been facing tremendous political pressures, and a strategy of "silence" seems to have taken root. Silence can be understood as "bystander complicity" but is also justified by leaders as a form of pragmatism of managing under the radar to do the hard labor required by values of diversity, inclusion, equity, and social change rooted in foundations of the American university while avoiding stirring political pots.

What Jose described was certainly the atmosphere in institutions with which I am familiar. I've followed heated debates about the need for universities to maintain neutrality to foster an atmosphere of free speech and debate, even among unpopular and unexpected opinions. This approach was also challenged by expectations professed by some critics that some moral and human rights crises require institutions of higher education to take a clear stand.

These debates continue to bubble and now (at the time when I am writing this book in 2023–24) have recently burst into ferocious confrontation over global conflicts.[8] They become especially complex when a faculty's academic leader happens to be from the country being ostracized, as has been my case in the aftermath of the October 7, 2023, Israel-Hamas war.

Interviewees also shared how cultural differences in conversation and argumentation styles impact their effectiveness in administrative roles. For example, my Israeli *dugri* conversational style (i.e., direct, "in your face," transparent discourse) can be perceived sometimes as rude and hurtful in the American context, yet can also be valued for its transparency and honesty.[9] A common joke among Israelis is that when two Israelis meet in the street and say, "We should have lunch sometime," the expectation is that they will get their calendars out and set a date right there and then. However, when two Americans meet and tell each other, "We should have lunch sometime," it can be interpreted as "Don't hold your breath—there is little chance this will ever happen."

By way of contrast, Canadian interviewees claimed that they are less confrontational than Americans and often do not raise their voices, so they don't feel they have the skills needed to address heated discussions; on the other hand, their presence in such meetings can have a soothing effect on a potentially escalating conflict. Asian female interviewees talked about having been socialized not to speak up and to suppress their individuality, so they are often perceived, mistakenly, as if they have nothing to contribute to faculty discussions and committees' deliberations.

Juan (Mexico to the United States), however, elaborated on the unique strengths of his immigrant status for leadership. He shared,

> One of the values I have as an immigrant is to be able to make it. [...] I also find that because I tend to be tactical because I am an immigrant, I think one becomes a very adaptive person. You are called to be adaptive all the time. I find that the university bureaucracies respond really well to that [...] so this immigrant characteristic has helped me a lot to live in the university. [...] So too my willingness to think that my way of thinking and doing is not the norm.

Similarly, Avi (Israel to the United States) talked about adaptability in terms of "navigation" as he discussed his observation of the differences between his Israeli background and the need to learn to navigate the American one. But he turned around to see it as a significant professional benefit for him:

> It informed my perspective of my own work and how I understand human behavior—we're in a constant mode of navigation. We're constantly navigating things. And so, I'm interested personally in how I can help people navigate. How do I create tools, how do I connect them with information, and so forth? I can help them navigate different kinds of challenges.

In his interview (above), Juan continued to share another of his unique assets: "One of the funny things about being a director is that the immigrant narrative really resonates with donors. I think a lot of donors figure themselves as pulling themselves up by their bootstraps. [...] I think when they hear my rags-to-riches, in a sense, my immigrant story, it resonates with them. [...] I have found it very easy to talk to donors once we establish similar values."

Not WEIRD

Given that the academic world is a very global enterprise—that is materialized through participation in international journals, conferences, transnational collaborations, and exchange programs, among others—academic immigrants serve as stimulators, knowledge brokers, and facilitators of many such endeavors.

Viewed from a macro perspective, collectively, academic immigrants contribute significantly to the dismantling of the WEIRD (Western, Educated, Industrialized, Rich, Democratic) dominance of Western academia.[10] Most of what we know today about social life around the world originates from Western and industrialized cultures and worldviews. A psychologist called it "the neglected 95%."[11] For example, in my field of children and media, we have observed that the vast majority of publications come from the Western world and focus on White middle-class children.[12] While our research seems to lack generalizability to broad swaths of the globe, there is often, nevertheless, an assumption of universality. We all understand the world through our own cultural and local lenses, and we assume that others' perceptions and values are similar to our own. Migrant academics are catalysts for changing the nature of research in the social sciences and integrating the rest of the world into scholarship, teaching, and leadership.

From a micro perspective, engaging in scholarship, teaching, and leadership is also a way of expressing pride in one's identity, demonstrating and celebrating self-worth, and nourishing a sense of belonging. Even when one is an "other" in a foreign country, one brings his or her sense of belonging through infusing it in one's academic work. The issue of belonging, and "home," is the topic of the next chapter.

6

The Home

Where Is Home for
Academic Immigrants?

"Where Do We Belong? What Is Home?"

Reflections on the complicated concept of "home," not as a physical space but as a sphere of belonging deeply embedded in issues of identity, nationality, culture, and nostalgia, were a focus of a great deal of contemplation during the interviews. "Where is home?" is one of the questions I asked all of the interviewees during our conversations. Interviewees' responses were contemplative and led to reflections on "what is home," "how do you nourish a sense of home," and the emotional labor of a quest for home and a longing for a sense of belonging that may not even be possible. The varied answers to this question turned out to be a lot more nuanced and complicated than I had expected.

Rich literature already exists on the concept of "home" in a host of disciplines including sociology, geography, cultural studies, and housing studies, among others. It is understood to be a multidimensional concept incorporating the real and the imagined, the place and the idea, that requires multidisciplinary research.[1] More specifically, in migration studies, special attention has been paid to the need for people transitioning from one culture to another to search for a new sense of home, conceptualized as the process of "homing."[2]

Home is characterized as a space (often anchored also in a concrete place) that provides a sense of familiarity, grants a feeling of safety, and allows the immigrants to feel they have regained control over their lives. Nourished by memories of a past home that was left behind and aspiring for a new home in the present and perhaps well into an imagined future, being at home is forever a fluid sensibility that is strongly related to a sense of belonging and well-being. Since the home is also related to the concept of homeland, it strongly intersects with the many dimensions of identity, including those related to gender, race, religion, and class. Home is thus a multifaceted and intersectional "idea," a locus of emotions and aspirations, rather than just a physical space of the residence, although that dimension is of great importance as well. Furthermore, home is also created and maintained via a host of social relationships as it is intertwined with the world around it.[3] More specifically, communities of migrants who share the experience of losing a home and a resulting sense of estrangement search through social relationships that they have in common.[4]

What seems to be absent from many of the theoretical discussions is an empirical biographical account of the voices of immigrants that share their longing, searching, interpreting, aspiring, and giving meaning to what home means to them, in their own words. This chapter attempts to help fill this gap.

Where Are You From?

From the point of view of the receiving country, the exploration of "where is home" was very often translated into the "where are you from" question. Many of my interviewees mentioned this spontaneously, as a constant reminder to them of their otherness, of society's assumption about their belonging somewhere else, of being strangers in their midst. The "Where are you from" questions were often triggered by detecting a foreign accent, thus confronting the immigrant with a sense of deficiency. Thus, accents were perceived most commonly as markers of otherness, and even as markers of inferiority. Such questions can be interpreted as a form of invisible boundary-drawing practices of belonging to a particular social space, in our particular context, a university setting.[5]

Whether the question was an expression of genuine curiosity and interest in the academic immigrant roots and personal history or an attempt to put the immigrant in his or her "place," it became a symbol of alienation and a source of great irritation to many interviewees. Examples in the interview were in abundance. While this is a common experience of immigrants and not at all unique to academic immigrants, what was experienced as unexpected was the fact that it was part of their everyday interactions on campuses with colleagues and administrators.[6] It was strongly perceived as a behavioral practice that marginalized them and made them feel less respected and supported in their higher education institutions. Tamir (Israel to the United States), for example, said, "You are always an outsider when you have an accent. People ask you where you're from and, you know, you can write a whole new article about types of 'Where are you from,' I'm sure. But yes, you're not fully integrated. You learn to accept that." And Jose (Argentina to the United States) shared: "People say, 'Oh, where are you from?'—it's a marker of otherness."

Similarly, Enrichetta (Italy to the United States) explained: "I start speaking, and of course I have an accent that is not a U.S. accent. So then, I get this question, 'Oh, but where are you from?' So at first, I would say, 'Well, I'm from Italy.' Now I say, 'I'm from the Midwest' [laughs]. [...] But how I feel internally... I don't know; it's really a mess."

Jennifer, who moved from one English-speaking culture to another (the United Kingdom to the United States), still experienced the same sentiment: "People say, 'Oh, where are you from?' When I first was here, it was very hard—and I'm sure, you know, everyone who has some sort of accent experiences this—'Oh, you have an accent. Where are you from?' And when I first was here, I found that very hard because it was just another reminder that I was an outsider."

In some cases, the interviewees' narratives placed the "Where are you from" question in the center of a much deeper discussion of their sense of being not only othered but also stereotyped. George (Romania to the United States), for example, conveyed this frustration:

> When people perceive that you have some kind of an accent, they start asking you, sometimes nicely, sometimes the question, "Where are you from?" or "What kind of accent is this very nice accent?" And you say "Romania" and they have a perception of that part of the world. So ten years ago, people had the perception, "Oh, it's the country of Nadia Comaneci, the gymnast." Or, "Oh, Dracula

country." Or, "It's the country of dictator Nicolae Ceausescu." Or "Oh, former communist country, okay." So they kind of, in their mind, [. . .] put you in a certain drawer in which whatever you do, whatever you are now, however, you are expressing yourself, however you are trying to make a discussion, they will put you in the label: Romania.

Gisela (Germany to the United States) shared her frustration:

I think people notice my accent and sooner or later they will ask, "Where are you from? Where are you originally from?" And sometimes, I'm really tired. I don't want to answer that question. Because I don't think it really matters, and people don't realize there's a long history to it. And I don't always want to explain. Because if I say, "I'm German," they come with beer and the sausages and Munich. I have nothing to do with Bavaria. I have nothing to do with West Germany. I have a complicated history and I don't feel like talking about it all the time.

In Yee's narrative (Hong Kong to the United Kingdom), the stereotyping was connected to plain racism when she related,

Most people will usually ask, you know, "What's your background? Where are you from? Where's your family from?" kind of things. So I would say, "Hong Kong." [. . .] All through the time I've been in the U.K., that's always almost the first question people ask. And you know, it gets really kind of annoying. And if I say I am from London, they wouldn't believe it, and they'll say, like, "Oh, no, but you've got an accent. Oh, where's your family from?" You know, that sort of thing. [. . .] I always think that, you know, the racism in this country, how long have I been here now? This is, gosh, over thirty years, right? I've been here. And I think—I feel that people are certainly mostly in kind of cities or metropolitan centers are more aware. So, if they have kind of racist ideas, they know, usually, mostly, not to say something. But I don't think it's ever really gone away. For me, sometimes, I feel like maybe it's just more hidden. For example, the virus [COVID-19 pandemic] so far, I've heard a lot of comments and incidents where people have been attacked because they are Asian-looking. So, it rears its head very easily, I think. Still.

Even when accepting the possibility that the question does not necessarily always express marginalization, several of the interviewees continued to feel a strong sense of offense and a significant emotional toll. Yerim (South Korea to the United States), for example, shared her attempts to process such encounters:

> And I remember sitting at a coffee shop, working. And an older gentleman came up to me and said, "Oh, you look really exotic. Where are you from?" And I started to lie at that point, and I said, "I'm from California." Because that's where I was from at that point. And then he just kept asking, "No, you don't look, you know, American." And so, I got so upset and I remember trying to tell my colleague in the same department. You know, she was super nice. And so, I try to tell her, "You know, this happened. You know, I just cannot believe it." And she kind of, again, tried to help me by saying, "But do you think that the person might have been trying to be nice to you and get to know you?" And I'm like, "I know, I know, they didn't have any malicious intent or anything. But it contributes to me feeling never accepted here." And so, at one point, I just couldn't explain—because all my colleagues were also White. And they were super nice. And yet, there were certain limits for them to understand truly what was going on internally. And so, I ended up kind of deciding that I won't speak about things like this, and that's okay. But of course, that, in a way, made it harder that I couldn't express these feelings.

With time, the participants in the study learned to cope with these questions, either by accepting them as inevitable, becoming indifferent, or actually digging deeper into their home country's identity. Xiao (China to the United States) has learned not to be apologetic for his Chinese origins in such interactions: "People ask me, 'Where are you from?' I know what they want to ask, but I always tell them 'I'm from Illinois.' But sometimes, if I feel like it, I tell them 'Originally I'm from China.' Because that's what they really want to know, actually. [. . .] I know what the problems are. But there are problems everywhere in the world. No matter what country you are living in. You have to cope with that."

Similarly, Nathan (Israel to the United States) found himself reasserting his Israeli identity:

A student of mine—and other people who were friends and frank and honest were telling me, "You know, you look like a White person, and then suddenly you open your mouth and there is this accent and it just disorients people." And so, you know, in the U.S., everybody's asking—the first question is, "Where are you from?" I thought it was just, "Are you from Illinois? Are you from Connecticut? Are you from, you know, New Jersey?" But there is this sense of putting you in a box. Like, "Where are you from?" So, I need to say that I'm from Israel. So, I do feel that I'm very Israeli. In whatever identification, eventually, I would say I'm Israeli. That's the most central part of my personality and everything is shaped by, like, Israeli culture. But definitely feeling, like, you know, not belonging.

Many of the interviewees recognized that the "Where are you from" questions were often genuine questions of interest and curiosity, but nonetheless found them to be mechanisms of stereotyping, as Mona (Kuwait to the United States) explained: "If you tell people you're Arab, they automatically assume that they know everything about you. [. . .] It's kind of annoying. But I now know that sometimes it's a way that people want to connect with you. They are trying to have small talk."

The discussion of "Where are you from" questions led me to dig more deeply into interviewees' thoughts about "home."

Where Is Home?

Reflections on the concept of "home"—not as a concrete space, but as an abstract focus of identity and belonging, were central to the interview, so I asked all interviewees, "Does the home country or host country feel like 'home'"? For some, the answer was one or the other; for others, both; and yet for a few, neither. My participants seem to be spread over a continuum of relationships with a sense of "home." On one end of the continuum, there was the host country, and on the other end, the home country. In the middle were the cases that felt that both were their homes.

Interestingly, two smaller groups of participants fell outside of the continuum: on one hand, the ones who felt they had no sense of home anywhere; and on the other hand, those who felt that the globe was their home. Each choice carried with it a different sensibility and set of assumptions and an attitude toward the everyday experiences of their professional lives.

Home and Home: Double Lives

Interviewees who defined themselves as having two homes, both the host country and the home one, describe themselves as living double lives of sorts. They would often describe interactions they have with colleagues in the host country when telling them they are "going home," that is, to visit their home country; and yet, when they are ready to return to the host country, they tell their family members and friends that they are "going home." Jozef (Belgium to the United States) shared such an example:

> I noticed it today, here, at the conference. I had a very restless night because—how do I put this into words? But I kind of—I run into someone, they said, "Yeah, that's the problem if you're an immigrant. You'll never belong to either culture ever again." And I think I'm at that stage. I don't miss Belgium at all. Maybe a few types of food, but I'm, I'm fine with that. I don't miss any people, really. I've always been a bit of a loner, so, I don't mind that. I think somebody said, "You're at the stage where you sound as if you've integrated but not yet assimilated." I think that's, that's what I feel. So, I feel at home. If I—if we go, like, if I fly back, it feels like going home. [...] Yeah, fly back to the university town, it feels like going home.

This was the most common narrative expressed in the interviews, by some 80 percent of my participants. They played expected roles within their departments, but they identified themselves by their home-country citizenship: "I am English living in New York." "I am a Brazilian living in Sweden." "I am a New Zealander living in the U.K." "I am an Indian with a permanent residency in the U.S." Constantinos (Greece to the United States) expressed a sentiment shared by many: "I'm very happy that I'm here, but I'll always consider myself Greek. Nothing is going to change that—[...] It's the homeland." Similarly, Avi (Israel to the United States) expressed his strong attachment: "I feel I am very attached to Israel. You know, it's the most beautiful country in the world. And I still like the people."

Others accepted that while their identity is clearly linked to their homeland, they were developing a second one toward their host country. Cristina (Brazil to Portugal), for example, explained, "I am hybrid. I explain that I have a layered identity. I moved here when I was twenty-one. So, most of my adult life has been here." And Nadya (Bulgaria to the United States) said, "I still if you asked me how I see myself, it would be as a Bulgarian citizen. But I am also heavily invested in the U.S. It's not my country of citizenship, but it is my home. I still don't feel quite American, but I feel like my own life is very much intertwined with what's going on in this country, and it's probably where I'm going to be spending the rest of it."

Meena (India to the United States) summarized it clearly: "Even though home, the word 'home,' refers to many spaces. So, when I'm in India, home is here [the United States]. When I'm here, India is home. [. . .] Yeah, it's home and home. So, it's the classic diasporic existence where you're home in multiple places."

Interestingly enough, only a few interviewees used a hyphenated identity, and all were among those immigrating to the United States, where such use is common among second-generation immigrant families (e.g., Juan identified as Mexican-American; Hassan as Iranian-American; Ning as Chinese-American; Jae-Joon as Korean-American), emphasizing their original identity first and the adopted one second. Of note is also the fact that although many of my interviewees managed their dual identities with ease, accepted their unique "edge" as outsiders in their new home, and were not lamenting the loss of a prior life, even feeling estranged from it, none of them felt completely integrated and becoming a member of the mainstream in their respective societies.

No Home: Alien in the Host Country

In contrast to interviewees who managed their double-life sensibilities, other interviewees believe that they never found a home in their institutions, they are not appreciated, they have always been treated suspiciously as "others," or their opinions are dismissed or considered marginal. They mostly learn to accept it as the price to pay for the benefits of their immigration story (for any of the 3Ps reasons) but live in a constant state of longing for a sense of belonging. Many continue to relate to their home country as their symbolic home, even after being away from it for many years. Their national and cultural identity remains the force they perceive as "home."

For example, Teresa (Puerto Rico to the mainland United States) shared the heartache she is experiencing as an alien:

> There are many stereotypes and things that I'm not used to [in the United States]. I'll give you an example. I'm a bit darker, but when I'm in Puerto Rico, I get really, really dark. And, you know, I've got curly hair, et cetera. My husband was very, very White. But in Puerto Rico, you don't care. But here, you talk a lot about Black and White, but over there, you don't. [...]
>
> And, after [hurricane] Maria, it became very obvious. They [the United States] told us we're not part of them. [...] There's a lot of people who have this fantasy that they think that they are part of the United States. But they're not. The United States tells us we're not. [...]
>
> That's one of the things I always tell my students. I'm always a minority. I came here almost forty years ago. It's a hard situation. But it's a hard situation for every immigrant anyway. Somebody on Facebook just put something about "Oh, I'm here in Peru, and it's so hard to go back and, you know, my children live in the United States and my family is here," you know, and I responded, "That's what the brave immigrant does. They know from the beginning that their heart is always gonna be heartbroken forever. [...] So it's just like you're still finding your space at this age.

The sense of loss that comes with immigration does not pass over academic immigrants, even when their move was one of choice and acceptance, as Mina (India to the United States) told me:

> It was a very emotional day for me when I physically had to return my Indian passport... very sad day for me. So even though everybody was saying, "Congratulations on becoming a U.S. citizen," I didn't take it as a congratulation. I felt like, "I'm doing this for my husband, I'm doing this for my family." [...] I would have still wished to go back to India.

Yerim (South Korea to the United States) also feels like an alien in her new environment, and when having to choose citizenship, her decision is quite clear:

> I would say, I am always going to say I'm Korean. Based on my citizenship status and what my passport looks like. Since I can't be a

dual-citizen, I have to pick a side, I guess, technically speaking. But I still do feel like I'm a Korean permanently living in America. So, culturally, I can say that I'm American. But again, moments like that, when people ask me, like, "Oh, are you actually from America?" Those are moments I realize, "Oh, that's right. I can't fully say that I'm American fully, culturally, even though I can pretend to be." And so, I think that's a reason why I keep just telling myself, "Okay." It's a coping mechanism that I'm Korean, and it's okay if I'm not fully accepted as one of the Americans.

Sometimes the realization that the "true" home is, after all, the home country comes at a moment of social crisis in their host country. Such, for example, was the case for several of my interviewees living in the United Kingdom during the process of Brexit. Paula (Germany to the United Kingdom) shared such an example:

> I kind of, I had to think about "Okay, is it because I'm German?" You know, is the [difference in maintaining physical] distance because I'm German? Or is it just because of my personality? If I don't understand something, is it because I'm different from being German? And it fascinates me because, I mean, we all constantly think about, you know, national stereotypes. And we assume national culture.
> And, actually, personally, I believe we're making way too much of that. Those differences are very personal and not necessarily national [. . .] but I've never felt British. But I think this is, you know, because London really is a cosmopolitan city. And so, I always loved London, but I never really felt British because I never experienced that Britishness that much. [. . .] I was quite proud that nobody could tell I'm German. But when other people in the U.K. started taking British citizenship [out of fear of losing their jobs because of Brexit], strangely enough, I felt, "No, I can't do this. I'm German. I'm not British." And it was always very clear that I would never, ever, take British citizenship, even though I could have had dual citizenship. Because I thought, "Well, but I don't feel British. And I don't want to swear allegiance to the queen." That feels really odd and very wrong.

In a few cases, my interviewees accepted their status as aliens and had no desire to fully integrate, as Hyejin (South Korea) to the United States) said somehow in defiance:

> I don't have a desire to integrate. No, not at all. I don't know about the culture, and I'm not interested to know. I feel very alien. [...] Of course, there are pros and cons of working here versus there. After comparing these pros and cons, I made a decision and I'm here. But I have a dream that I want to, you know, be faculty there. [...] I am Korean. I am not American. I can never be an American. I don't think I will ever get rid of this Korean accent. I hate when people call me [a mispronunciation of name] ... I always fix the pronunciation of my name. Because I am Korean. And that's my name.

Just as in the "Where are you from" exchanges, being pointed out as different served my interviewees to strengthen their original identity and attach themselves even more to their home country, as in the case of Lilian (Canada to the United States): "I think that living in the U.S. makes me feel more Canadian than I ever felt living in Canada. [...] It feels like Canada is also somewhere I could always go back to. It feels like a safeguard."

No Home: Alien and Alien

While time did not necessarily make my interviewees less alien in their host country, it did make some feel more alien in their original home country. To contrast them with the Home and Home group, they are an "Alien and Alien" group. Such, for example, was the story of Gisela (Germany to the United States):

> People here always detect that I'm different. That I'm Yugoslavian, Danish, Swedish, German. And then, when I'm in Germany, people joke that I'm American. And so, I feel like you are jaded on both sides in some way. And you are lost, right? [...] My husband is American, he doesn't speak German, and he understands very closely what my life is like, but he will never understand my East German culture. And my close friends in Germany will never understand my American life.
>
> So, I think there sometimes is a little bit of sadness that you are not belonging to anything completely anymore. [...] It's mixed

because the positive is that I'm super privileged. I have two citizenships—who has that? And I can move freely around the world. I can research and study what I like. I have a great job and great colleagues. And I'm a success story also in the sense that my parents are working class and I'm now what we call in German "education bourgeoisie." And so, that is the same thing, that my parents are very proud of me. But they don't understand my world, right?

Mayur (India to the United States) experienced a similar loss:

The plan was to actually go back to India [...] And I think, maybe by the end of my second year, it was clear that there was a good possibility I would actually stay here instead of going back to India. And I kind of remember that at the end of my second year, I visited India—and that was my first time going back to India since I left—and realizing that almost unknowingly or subconsciously I kind of, I don't know, shifted the culture.

So, the same culture in India was now a little bit foreign to me, and I kind of started thinking, oh man, now I don't fit in here as much as well. And I could see that the more time I spent away from India, this was going to just keep getting harder. And that's what actually happened. That I found myself not fitting as well in the same culture.

The realization that places, people, and culture were not what they remembered and, so, their home country is changing seems to have been unexpected and overwhelming for many of the interviewees. Each experience of the return home honed the realization that you "cannot step into the same river twice" because things that seem to be the same are actually constantly changing.

This feeling "out of place" in one's own homeland that has been documented in other studies and shared by many of my participants (a theme we will return to in chapter 8) was also captured by Armin (Barbados to the United States):[7]

So, that sense of being sort of slightly off-balance is my disposition. Barbados now, I can never return to the way that I was before. I read the Barbados newspapers all the time. I did this research project in which Barbados was a central part of it. I returned to Barbados in-depth trying to understand it through its educational system. I would say that I'm still in search of something in terms of identity that I've not arrived at and probably never will. And I think at this stage in my life, I'll have to accept it.

If you scratch me deeper, I think I would say that I'm Barbadian. After all these years. But if you scratch that deeper, I think I couldn't say that with any final security. 'Cause, you know, you know that you're also outside of that formation. Or whatever it's become because it's become something else since I left. We go there every year, sometimes two or three times. I retain a strong relationship with my family there [...] but it's not the same thing. It's not the same thing as when my mother was alive. [...]

As an immigrant, I feel like this is a society I would never be able to integrate into. And that I accept it. And don't necessarily see it as an ultimate loss. Maybe in some ways, it gives me certain affordances. [...] Maybe if I came here when I was younger, I would have understood it better. And because of training, so many things had been sort of scorched into my consciousness, that it almost didn't allow for maybe a full openness to the transition to another identity. So, you sort of inhabit this tumultuous place of being both part of something and outside of it.

Finally, I want to share a long passage from Maya's (Israel to the United Kingdom) narrative, since it resonates so strongly with some of my own experiences of managing dual identities, being torn between the love of my home country and the desire to disassociate from it, and the deep sense of uprooting that becomes one's core experience:

> I think over the years, the opposite also happens. You come [to Israel] and you growingly feel like a tourist. Also, of course, you finally, you know, you feel you don't belong there either. But I, if I'm honest, it's also, I'm feeling less and less, you know, it's not a place that I would call necessarily home today. [...] but as far as my feelings are concerned [about life in U.K. academia], I feel a stranger, and I feel a minority. And I feel, you know, I don't feel part of whatever it is that is represented to be the dominant hegemonic, powerful culture. But I think you're often being read as such because visually, nothing suggests...

And it's become very convoluted. I feel, recently, with a lot of, you know, with the plight of a lot of, particularly women of color in academia. That I feel sometimes I kind of almost don't have, my voice is not legitimated as a voice of the minority. And I think it's further complicated by the Israeliness because of the Israeli association with occupation and so on, there's nothing that is, you know, it's not that I want to claim the badge of the disempowered or the impoverished. But I do feel sometimes that I contribute to the discussion as much perspective of someone who is in the margins. And it's not, and I can't claim it or I can't articulate it. So, I don't know how much sense it makes.

I think because I'm White, and visually, I don't come across as a stranger or foreigner, I think that's something that often complicates things in the way you are being read. It's only as soon as you open your mouth that your accent discloses that you are not from here. . . . And it's interesting because I feel that at least at the university, there's a lot of very complicated, quite charged identity politics around also voice and who is allowed to say things and who is not, where I feel that, how shall I say it? Yeah, I feel I'm in an awkward place in this regard because as far as my feelings are concerned, I feel like a stranger, and I feel a minority. And I feel, you know, I don't feel part of whatever it is that is represented to be the dominant hegemonic, powerful culture.

This rich narrative combines the complexity of being White and thus not recognized as a minority but at the same time feeling marginalized and othered, particularly as an Israeli torn between a born identity and a growing alienation from the current politics of the country. Many academic immigrants, like Maya, are caught in racial dynamics and political trends that they do not identify with, just because of their perceived identity. They find themselves expected to explain their home country's wrongdoing, and unable to disassociate themselves from those expectations. The result is that they often shy away from any mention or discussion of politics related to their home country, hiding their roots on the website or in conversations. But, sometimes, the opposite happens too, as some of the colleagues shared: they find themselves trying to explain and justify actions that they would have been the first to demonstrate against if still living in their home country.

In email correspondence I had with Yufeng, a young scholar (China to the United States), who related to one of my earlier published articles on this study, he wrote to me in an email (February 5, 2024, shared with his permission):

> Another point I want to mention is the prevalent "home-no-home" feeling I similarly experienced during fieldwork in China, where my family's "home" is. In other words, this sense of alienness is embodied when I'm returning "home." When I spoke with informants in my hometown, I was similarly othered as someone representing the US or a foreign institution. Even though we spoke the same dialect and shared past experiences, people were cautious about what they could share with me. Amid the worsening China-US geopolitical tensions, I find myself becoming increasingly distant from both "China" and "the US," and I foresee the autonomy of my in-between space being increasingly threatened by such tensions.

Similar sentiments surfaced in other interviews of participants from countries that have contentious relationships with the United States, especially China, who felt simultaneously alien both in their original homeland and in their host country.

The mention of the "in-between space" invokes the concept of the Third Space, the hybrid liminal space in between cultures—in this study, between the original homeland culture and the newly adopted culture.[8] The two have complicated relationships. They conflict with each other, they intersect, they merge into each other, and in the process, they create a vibrant, dynamic, and ever-changing cultural space. While the Third Space has been largely applied to the study of postcolonialism, it is also a highly productive theory to employ in studies of immigration, as I have learned from my case studies. However, what surfaced in the Chinese examples is a concern that the hybrid Third Space may be in danger of losing its comfort and vitality when the two other spaces (the Chinese and the U.S.) are in conflict with each other. Similar sentiments have been expressed by Israeli immigrants, like myself, in the aftermath of the October 7, 2023, massacre and the outbreak of another phase of the intense violent conflict that followed. Suddenly the Third Space thinned out and lost its feeling of security and comfort. This seems to be the feeling Yufeng wrote about in the remainder of his email:

> This year marks my 7th year in the U.S. Like many of your interviewees, I can't categorize myself as Chinese, Singaporean, or American, but paradoxically, I might be categorized as all three. In thinking with Homi Bhabha, I occupy this in-between third space that's both a blessing and a curse, as you articulated well in your article.[9] Embracing this multiplicity and fluidity, I feel as if there's no "true" or "authentic" core self for me, as I'm ontologically fragmented and relational.

Yufeng's use of the word "fragmented" in regard to his sense of self resonated very strongly with the way I was feeling, an experience I will return to in the closing postscript of this book.

Home in the World

In a dozen cases, academic immigrants did not attach themselves to "place," but their identity was more one of being an intellectual, home being academia itself, the sphere focused on the pursuit of scholarship and education in the universal sense. Interviewees suggested that as academics, intellectual life replaces the desire for home, providing an anchor of existence that "place" may offer others. They see themselves as citizens of the world of thought, detached from the constraints of geographical boundaries. They would pick up, leave for a new challenge, and believe they would land easily on their feet anywhere in academia. Meena (India to the United States) said it more directly: "I identify as a citizen of the world. I do not have any loyalty to an artificial construct called a nation-state. [. . .] What is more important to me are people whom I can identify with and share a worldview with."

Anna (Cyprus/Greece to the United Kingdom) became very emotional when discussing her torn identity. She said, "My core identity, I don't think I would define it based on nationality. [. . .] Of course, I'm Greek, I'm Cypriot, you know, I'm European. I would never say I'm British. But again, I'm a citizen of the world. I'm a socialist. An internationalist. All of these things."

Other interviewees explained that national identity is arbitrary. Lars (the United States to Singapore) said, "It's all arbitrary. I don't have any sense of national identity, not at all. My son, I think of raising him as a citizen of the world." Others, like Xiao (China to the United States), said that the earth is their home, rather than their nation. They brought up ideological perspectives, such as the view by Florence (the United States to Canada):

> I started to really see myself as a citizen of the world more than an American. [...] I've always felt that country borders are highly problematic [...] nationalism, exceptionalism, xenophobia, just so many problems. And I never really saw myself as an American first when I was traveling the world. I saw myself as a person, you know, who was relating to other people in the world.

A few explained the benefits of detaching from an identity anchored in a particular construct. For example, Doina (Romania to the United States) shared,

> I have always thought of myself as international. In some sort of a weird way, I liked my status when I had no status. [...] It was a neither here nor there situation that was not convenient administratively and perhaps less than convenient financially but was a sort of a strange freedom of thinking and freedom to invent your own ways of doing things in its uniqueness. [...] And I have always considered myself a citizen of the world.

The privilege of traveling, which comes with secured positions in academia, was mentioned in close relationship to the sense of global citizenship. For example, Okeke (Rwanda to the United States) said, "I tend to define myself as a multicultural person. Having a chance to travel a lot, you kind of develop like a different software in your mind."

Eddy (Europe to Israel) admitted, "I knew I would enjoy being a foreigner, you know, in-between. [...] I want to remain in between. I want to enjoy the possibility of moving from one place to the other. [...] I travel all the time. And for me, it's amazing."

And Cosmas (Nigeria to the United States) shared,

> I like exploring. I don't consider myself somebody to be confined to one country. I've always seen myself at the international level. [...] I always had a flair for things international. [...] I don't see myself as an outsider. I mean, even if I were to go to, let's say, Sweden, tomorrow, I

wouldn't also see myself as an outsider. [...] Because I keep saying that I like to be an international person. [...] We have a saying in Nigeria that "wherever you go is your home."

Home and COVID-19

In several interviews conducted remotely during the COVID-19 crisis, discussions of the concept of home turned into concrete reflections and decision-making. Where do I feel safe? Where do I want to be if things get out of control? Who will take care of my elderly parents if I am not there? Where do I want to die, be mourned, buried, or cremated, if this is to be my fate? What if I make a decision too late and I won't be able to travel to get there in time?

Suddenly, complicated immigration arrangements and compromises related to mixed partnerships, home ownership, employment, health care, children, and elderly parents were all challenged. Urgently, the concept of "home" reignited and, all too often, begged for very concrete decision-making. Some academics rushed to their home country to take care of their parents, to guarantee better health care, or to move to a rural environment. Others stayed put, as there was too much to lose by going back to their homeland. In doing so, they remained emotionally torn by loss of psychological comfort knowing they could always go for a visit. Now they couldn't.

I, too, found myself struggling with the concept of "home." I canceled airline tickets to a family event in Israel that summer. I had confidence and hope that eventually, I would be able to travel again, but what does it say about the future? About getting old and becoming vulnerable? About the day when going "home" is not going to be an option anymore—due to age and health, climate change, war, or another pandemic? Will I ever see "home" as colored by my childhood memories, enjoy Mediterranean smells, taste familiar foods, hear Hebrew spoken everywhere, walk accustomed streets, and most importantly, hug all my loved ones—family members, friends, and former students? All these and others were omnipresent but still quite hypothetical types of questions before 2019. But COVID-19 has pushed them front and center. Now they become real. Now they matter.

COVID-19 challenged much of our understanding of home as a place of safety, when crossing its threshold has become an existential threat. The "stay home" guidelines around the world fueled discussions of the central role of the home, physically and symbolically, in the living experience of people.[10] Yes, on the one hand, quarantining away from "home" was uniquely uncomfortable for immigrants. Yet, on the other hand, COVID-19 and quarantining led all of us into unfamiliar and threatening existential domains, needing to cross psychological borders and not merely national ones.[11]

Belonging

"Belonging," "not-belonging," "longing to belong," and mourning a sense of belonging to something bigger than oneself surfaced as a central yearning in many of the interviews. "Home," in many ways, can be interpreted in their narratives as a locus of the lived experience of belonging, a state of being where one feels belonging to the social-cultural fabric of the environment in which one lives their life, both as an emotional state of being and as a reference to social and cultural integration or lack thereof. For many academic immigrants, especially those who see themselves as transnational, having multiple homes or being citizens of the world, belonging is multifaceted, or can be understood as multibelonging. Even when they are residing in their home country, they are not fully "home" again.[12]

Do I belong? This was a question many of my interviewees asked themselves, often unsolicited when discussing questions related to "home."

Mona (Kuwait to the United States) shared her thoughts about belonging as a community project when we met at an academic conference:

> I would say, not feeling like I belong, not knowing... definitely does affect my happiness. I mean, even last night. I was tired; I left the reception. And I was thinking about it. I was thinking, you know, some people call a conference a home conference. That was on my mind. [...] And, you know, over time, you just start to realize, like, maybe there are ways of belonging. Even—even at a conference. [...] Where do we belong? What is home? I think it's always on my mind in some ways. But I also started becoming maybe more proactive about developing a sense of home. You know? When you see people, you can say hi to them and they can say hi to you and over the years, you start to develop an understanding that they're going to be here [in

the conference]. And you see new people, and you start to realize that maybe these new people are actually asking themselves the same question that you're asking yourself, which is, "Do I belong?" And maybe simply being here, simply by being accepted. Simply by attending—simply your presence, is a way of telling others that they belong. And so, it's not only about you. It's about this idea of home as something that we work hard to create. And that we cannot only develop it for ourselves but also embrace others somehow.

What I have learned from my participants, including those quoted above, suggested that perhaps the question should be not "Where is home" but "What is home." I echo here other scholars who concluded that given the contested nature of the concept of home in the academic literature, it has come to be understood in multiple ways.[13] In my interviews, it is often colored by nostalgic sentimentality for the past, a strong sense of yearning for a home that once was (perhaps) and can never be found again. The answer to that question, however, is complex, fluid, and dynamic, just as the sense of belonging and cultural identities.[14] To quote Abraham Verghese in *Cutting for Stone*, "Wasn't that the definition of home? Not where you are from, but where you are wanted?"[15]

7
The Bridge

What Keeps Immigrants Connected?

"I Can't Do This Without Community"

Given that nostalgic longing for a home left behind and a constant sense of living double lives were dominant themes in the personal narratives of my participants, it was natural for the conversations to morph into their efforts to bridge their current existence with their cultural roots. When asked what you miss most about "home," the almost unanimous response was family and friends. "Home is where your loved ones are" seemed an axiom subscribed by all and requires no explanation. Among loved ones is where we feel a sense of security, belonging, support, and purpose. However, two other answers dominated the conversations about longing for home—food and language—so lovely, immediate reflections symbolizing the two realms of our existence, the physical and the mental. Both are intertwined with larger questions of identity and preservation of connections with their homeland culture, socializing, and connections.

Food

"My mother's food," "my culture's food," "special holiday foods," "street food"—all variations of food that are so emotionally tied to a sense of belonging to a family, a community, a culture—all of which invoke nostalgic memories of the past, as well as feelings of comfort and happiness. Food engages all five senses—taste, smell, touch, vision, and even hearing. That food is a fundamental experience of immigration situated within a complex web of identities, memories, and relationships, among others, has been established in scholarship from around the world.[1] Similarly, interviewees in this study described cooking their cultural foods at home, exploring local grocery stores in their host communities owned by ex-pats and restaurants serving their home food, attending social gatherings serving their food, and so forth. The availability of home food in the host country seems to play a significant role in anchoring a sense of belonging. Nevertheless, when asked, "What do you miss most about your home country," they would say, "The food." Rhi Won (South Korea to the United States) explained:

> I have lived here long enough to learn how to cook a lot of American dishes. I think I'm good at cooking. So, I can make all different types of American dishes, such as sandwiches, pasta, and even special occasion foods for Thanksgiving. But I still need to eat Korean food regularly. I guess that it's part of my identity. If I keep eating sandwiches only or salad only, French fries only, I feel too greasy . . . and I need to have spicy Korean food, such as spicy Korean rice cake or some Korean kimchi. So, I cook Korean food because my body desires it naturally. Whenever I miss Korea, I cook Korean food for myself.

Cosmas (Nigeria to the United States) also has some reservations related to American food: "You won't find me eating some of these things that are around here. You know, hamburgers, and I don't drink Coke, Sprite. So, no matter how much they advertise, they won't catch me. I prefer African food. Fortunately, you can get them everywhere."

Even those interviewees who have been living in their host country for decades are still making a special effort to celebrate cultural holidays via special foods, as Violeta (Chile to the United States) shared: "For the holidays in Chile, which are coming up next week, I'm going to make Chilean empanadas. [. . .] I will do the Chilean drink, which is pisco sour. [. . .] And music, too."

Antonio (Puerto Rico to the mainland United States), who left his homeland several decades ago, shared, "I am Puerto Rican, always

Puerto Rican. I've kept my identity. And I've kept that identity in my family, in the art that we have at the house, we kept the identity in the language that we speak and travel, the food, the cuisine. Although we're a lot on the healthier side than on the greasy, fatty side, but we're very much on the Puerto Rican cuisine as much as we can. I've never, ever left that."

Food is also a means to proactively share one's culture with diverse host colleagues as presented by Lior's example (Israel/United States to Singapore):

> I immediately noticed that in our team there were people from seven countries. And I said, "Let's celebrate our identities. And let's do it through food." They liked it, but nobody did anything until one day I just came to the office late with hummus, tahini, pita bread. And I said, "Let's eat." And I showed them how to eat. Since then, we went to a Myanmar restaurant, an Indonesian restaurant, Chinese and Filipino, and Indian and we had a blast. And every time somebody else is hosting. It makes you feel more integrated.

Satya (India to Sweden), who felt quite lonely and isolated, used Indian food to create a community for herself:

> I just loved my students. I would cook big Indian meals and I would invite them to my house. Part of it is also because I was alone, and I didn't know I was creating a community. [...] Whenever I used to send those emails—"It's the Hindu festival of worshipping the god of knowledge," because that's nonacademic, I would get no response. Sometimes, somebody would say, "Oh, thank you for the sweets." Because I would leave sweets in the staff room.

Examples in the participants' narratives are abundant. The many roles that food plays in traditions, family life, culture, and holidays are central to any observer of diasporic life and are beyond the scope of this book.

Language

Native language in all modalities (e.g., spoken, printed, broadcasted, digitized) was a very central indicator of "home" in the interviews, as it plays a central role, together with traditional rituals, holidays, festivals, clothing, and the like, in the construction of "imagined communities."[2] Imagined communities share a sense of belonging that transcends being physically present in each other's place. While this concept was developed to understand nations and nationalism, it resonates very strongly with the diasporic experience whose identity is closely attached to the nation-state left behind.

The ambience of one's native language is omnipresent immediately on visits to the home country, as was mentioned by many of the interviewees. Examples they cited include when the airport porter speaks to me, listening to the radio in the taxi, and especially with the enthusiastic welcome with which one is greeted by family members and friends.

Despite years of functioning in the host country's language, it never carries the power of the mother tongue. Furthermore, the host language always requires more cognitive labor, as described vividly by Maya (Israel to the United Kingdom):

> But I must say, that just being able to speak Hebrew and not think in English, just makes me realize, again, even though I've been living in London now for twenty years, how much work, how much labor, it is for me at least, to operate and live in English. And there's something in—I just feel so much less tired in some ways when I speak my mother tongue of the native language. [I feel that] my English is not polished enough. That's not the BBC accent. I'm not kind of versed in the humor and in the sarcasm. That's a feeling that over the years has been lessened, partly because I am in such an international environment. Partly because I've learned a lot of the codes. And still, when I go to these—have this kind of moments, I feel really, very uncomfortable.

Hassan (Iran to the United States) reflected on the loss of his native language over time and feeling that he is still not in full control of English when he shared, "I used to read in Farsi . . . but not anymore. They send me stuff from Iran, like clips from social media, but I don't have that much practice. I just donated my Farsi book to a mosque here. I am not anymore using my language. I speak Kurdish. I speak Farsi. I can read Arabic. These are languages that I knew when I came here [decades ago], and I didn't know a word of English. And I am still learning English."

Passing on one's native language to the children is a top priority for many of my interviewees as they seemingly hold on to the possibility of keeping their home environment as authentic to their roots as possible. Gaus (Pakistan to the United States) explained: "We speak Pashtu at home. It is important for me that my children maintain their ability to speak. I am Muslim, but for me, the religious part is not that important. I am not a practicing Muslim, but we keep the cultural and the linguistic parts."

Tanzoui (Cameroon to the United States) shared that in addition to English, he and his family speak at home two indigenous languages, pidgin and Mangaka, and he explained why it is important for him that his children maintain those linguistic skills: "It's important because of the assimilation of these educational and social and economic and cultural tendencies of this country. I am struggling to see that they can maintain a lot of it. So, they can at least know, just like I tried to understand my father and my mother. It's good for us to know about the language of where we came from and know a little bit [...] so that he can affiliate himself with my family members."

Okeke (Rwanda to the United States) also had strong convictions about the importance of knowing one's ancestors' language and yet was realistic about the challenges of teaching it at home:

> To me, the mother tongue is the language that your parents speak when you are born, so we were very shocked that suddenly they [the children] were speaking English. And then we tried to force them to learn the mother tongue, but they actually don't need it for the time being. And it's probably going to come on their own because that's the only thing we speak, me and my wife. So, I think when they grow up—like my daughter is actually paying more attention—and she understands a lot of things that we say. But she doesn't kind of produce speech.

Naturally acquiring a second language at home becomes more complicated and often impossible when the academic immigrant partners with a local person from the host country from a different ethnicity and background and the loss—while accepted as part of the compromise of immigration—is nevertheless mourned. The scholarship on language and culture is of course vast and complicated and is beyond the scope of this study, but suffice it to say for our purposes that language plays a significant role in the immigration experience. Some of my participants continued to make special efforts to teach their children their native language. Elena (Russia to the United States) describes such a situation:

> Both of us speak English between ourselves, so we speak to them [children] a lot in English. But when I'm by myself with them, I'm making sure that I speak in Russian and [the older child] now finally started to speak more because, you know, when there are several languages in the family, it takes longer. He speaks mostly in English, but I make sure to repeat it all the time in Russian, and I like that he makes those connections.

Nathan, her partner (Israel to the United States), adds, "I am speaking to them in Hebrew and English, because we speak English at home, so English is their major language. I'm trying as much as I can when I'm speaking one-on-one to them."

The challenge of passing on mastery of the native language to the children remains a great challenge to many. Violeta (Chile to the United States) expressed her frustration: "With my kids, I tried to speak to them in Spanish, but it got to be so hard. It was just marginalizing them. And after a while, I thought, 'You know, I can't do this without community. My husband doesn't speak Spanish; we don't know anybody else, basically.' So I gave up on that."

Similarly, Yee (Hong Kong to the United States) shared her family situation: "I have been trying to talk to my daughter in Cantonese since she was born, so she has a really good understanding of Cantonese and to some extent, Mandarin. But she just never uses it because her father speaks English, so I also speak English, and she goes to school in English, and so on. So it's really hard to get her to use those languages."

Juan (Mexico to the United States), in discussing his primary school–age son, shared:

> I used to talk to him in Spanish and to my wife in English. But there was a point where actually his English was so advanced, and his Spanish was not equally advanced, that made me realize that I would—I couldn't have the same relationship in Spanish with him that I could in English. So, humor and wordplay and explaining

difficult concepts and such, you know, we felt that I needed to go to English. So, I began in the last probably three years to speak Spanish to him maybe half of the time. But it is super important. And it's super hard. I admire anyone who has been able to raise bilingual kids. It's very hard.

Some parents who viewed the linguistic skills in a more holistic way as closely embedded in a more holistic transmission of culture to their children were more insistent and demanding of both themselves and their children to engage in a "double shift." Such, for example, was the narrative related by Mina (India to the United States):

> I am particular that he [son] should know my language. [...] It's like having a parallel school at home, as an immigrant, right? When you live a bi-culture life. So, I'm celebrating all the festivals because I want him to know that this is what we do. And teach him the language and teach him Indian music. [...] So, I feel that he has to do double shift, where he's doing all of the things that the American students are doing, then come back home, learn the other things. So when I take him back to India, then I want him to see "Okay, this is what it is. This is your home. You need to know your roots. [...] Be very clear. Because this is an important part of who you are."

Similarly, Xiao (China to the United States) explained,

> I try to familiarize them [the children] with things that are Chinese. Chinese food, Chinese music, and Chinese arts. I want them to choose by themselves. Both China and the U.S. have great literary traditions and writing, arts. I want them to learn both so that they can benefit from them. [...] I always tell my ten-year-old that "there are so many good things in China. Good books to read, good poems, and good novels. If you don't know Chinese or don't know how to read and enjoy, you will miss out on them. And you are going to regret it."

Regular family trips back to the country of origin to visit family are a typical means by which the language learning and cultural socialization of the children takes place, as described by Donia (Romania to the United States):

Our girls are Americanized kids to some extent. They have been through the education system here. They have friends. They have peer pressure. But the fact that they can come with me to Romania many summers, being back and forth. They speak Romanian fairly well. They both enjoy many aspects of Romanian culture and understand the differences between Romania and the U.S. We speak Romanian at home. We kind of mix and match sometimes too. We aren't making that clear language separation. And the girls can answer whatever they want. We never imposed. Whatever they feel more comfortable with.

The view expressed by Cosmos (Nigeria to the United States) was mentioned frequently by parents who wanted their children to be integrated into the new society and yet maintain their cultural roots, and expressed it very clearly when discussing language learning:

My house is a United Nations. My wife is from Kenya. I lived in Kenya, but I don't speak Swahili. So, we speak in English. And that had rubbed off on our daughter. You know, now it's like, we speak English. [. . .] It is very important for me that she maintains ties to Nigeria, but unfortunately, she doesn't speak the language. But she's a Nigerian as even is her name. [. . .] Yes, yes, yes, yes, completely [trying to raise her with an African identity]. And I'm not losing sight of the fact that she's also an American. So, we try to, you know, combine and use the best of two cultures.

Media

Our interviewees living a dual life is also present in their daily use of media. They function all day in the host country's language—while teaching, doing scholarship, and interacting with colleagues, as they often also integrate social media messages or checking news in their original country's languages. In their private lives, they "return home" to speak their native language, as well as to enjoy recreational reading, listen/read/view the news or pop music, or enjoy a TV drama. Doing so in one's native language becomes an immensely powerful reinvigorating force, creating a bubble of a different lived experience for immigrants.

Storytelling, as others have argued, in all of its forms, literary and mediated, allows the immigrant to create a sense of home and belonging regardless of the boundaries of geographical and embodied location.[3]

The central role of media for diasporic communities is a topic of interest in a variety of disciplines.[4] Like other themes central to media studies, immigrants, too, as consumers and producers of media, as well as immigrants' representations in the media, have been a focus of studies of the diasporic experience.[5] Media are integrated in the way diasporic communities imagine themselves and are imagined by others as well as the ways they connect to each other and to their home countries. The narratives of the academic immigrants revealed that their ability to use media to maintain their culture, language, interpersonal, and professional relationships, as well as to manage their sense of identity, was almost taken for granted.

Maintaining Interpersonal Connections

The ability to be connected instantaneously with family members and friends across the globe and to maintain close intimate relationships via digitized technologies was a key feature for the interviewees. "Of course," they related when asked about it, they keep in touch via instant messaging platforms with their aging parents, siblings, or colleagues (e.g., WhatsApp with various parts of the world, WeChat with China, Kakaoo with Korea, Viber with Greece) as well as Skype, Facebook, Instagram, and Twitter/X, as HyeJin (South Korea to the United States) explained:

> Being in a different country from where you were born, and then you still want to keep in touch with your personal relationships, like your parents, your younger siblings, your friends. Right? [. . .] Technology like FaceTime and all those instant messaging services, like Kakoo Talk, so nowadays I don't feel any more the distance because you know, you exchange videos and pictures and like, all the time.

Similarly, Lynn (the United States to Europe) shared,

> My sisters and I had a WhatsApp chat on our phone since I moved there, because WhatsApp was the one technology that we could use regardless of phone type. And it's just running all-day-long pictures,

jokes, comments, just everything—it hasn't stopped in eight years. So, I feel like, when I see my sisters, it's just an ongoing communication. [...] And my mother and father [...] I got them iPhones and got it all set up so they can Facetime me. And, so, my mother Facetimes me all the time.

Sharing life experiences across the globe and time zones is a common experience, as Edith (New Zealand to the United Kingdom) relates:

> I'm often using WhatsApp because I've got kind of my London, you know, Kiwi friends. We have a group on WhatsApp. Then I have my family on WhatsApp and various friends. And Instagram as well, people posting pictures on Instagram. So, you know, often I'll wake up in the morning, I'm just waking up, and I'll have a whole lot of messages that have come through from New Zealand overnight that might include, you know, gorgeous pictures or something and so on. But of course, it works the other way, right? I've been here, it's been a beautiful hot heat wave in the U.K., and so I'm getting pictures the other way.

Digital technological innovation has facilitated easy and inexpensive cross-geographical and national border connections (as long as they are not restricted by certain political regimes) that allow immigrants to remain in constant touch with their home families and friends.

Cultural Connections

A highly important function that the media serve for immigrants is the ability to immerse themselves in a symbolic ambience of the familiar home culture via the consumption of cultural products: Indian cricket matches and Bollywood movies, Korean pop and TV series, Irish Gaelic football, Israeli political satire, Nigerian Nollywood movies, and soccer matches—these are just a few of the examples brought up in the interviews.

As Xiaolan (China to the United States) shared, "When I watch TV soap operas or movies, I still prefer the Chinese. [...] First of all, the language, it's easier to catch up. And second, I mean, you can feel the connections. The background, the culture... you have more emotional echoes, connections with the characters... and also the cultural values, traditional Chinese values."

Similarly, Davide (Italy to the United Kingdom) was actively seeking Italian movies: "You know, watching Italian movies for me is a way of also kind of keeping in touch, knowing what's going on in Italian society. Watching movies is really a good way of understanding how society is changing.

Yerim (South Korea to the United States) consumed Korean content on a variety of media forms: "Thanks to the internet, thanks to YouTube and all of these things that are feeding me information that I need. And so, I do think that I'm keeping in touch with the cultural things. What's popular on social media and some of those basics."

Ikechukwu (Nigeria to the United States) felt a similar connection while watching soccer games: "It doesn't matter the time—If Nigeria is playing, I will watch it as long as it's on television. I will go to every length to find it and to watch it. My television package is actually chosen to make sure that I can watch as much as possible."

Watching movies and television series, listening to music, accessing cultural websites, enjoying memes on social media, and reading novels—all in the native language—were all typical examples of how the immigrants chose to remain connected to their roots. This is also how they found both cognitive and emotional refuges from the surrounding environment in which they often felt as "visitors," sometimes even as aliens, and most commonly, just mentally tired from normal everyday challenges at the university.

News

One particular genre of media content received significant attention in the interviews—news sources from the home country. To a large degree, consuming "news" (credible or suspicious, from a well-established newspaper website, television or radio channel, or diffused on social media) played an important role in helping the immigrants feel that they are informed, connected, and involved in what is happening at "home." But, at the same time, most of them also felt a strong need to keep up with the news of their new home country for a variety of reasons, chiefly to be informed for interactions with their colleagues and students. Some were just avid news consumers, such as Andres (Norway to the United States): "I actually read the Norwegian paper every day. Online, right? And I'm, you know, I enjoy the contrast between Norwegian politics and U.S. politics. But, I mean, yeah, I actually follow political developments, yeah, relatively broadly. I track what's happening in China, in India, in Italy, in Britain. Brexit."

Some of the participants structured their day around their news consumption habits. For example, Jon (the United Kingdom to the United States) shared,

> So, we start the day with *The Guardian* crossword. We subscribe to the British edition of *The Guardian*, which comes in overnight. So, I read it. Actually it's released at ten o'clock local time here. So, I kind of read tomorrow's headlines in *The Guardian* and dip into it. When we start the day in the gym at home, I normally put on CNN. [...] So we get a good dose of American politics to start the day. And I read, rather obsessively, the *New York Times* and the *Washington Post*. [...] Sometimes I get the VPN going and have the iPad, so watching the news, U.K. British News 24 in real-time. And, so, if there's something like an important debate or something, it's nice to have the British news as presented to the British.

Demetrios (Greece to the United States), too, follows both Greek and American sources of news: "I'm not a morning person, so when I get up in the morning, I do things that don't require a lot of interaction. So, I listen to NPR for some time, and I listen to Greek radio programs for some time as well while I'm doing email or having breakfast or heading out the door." Avi (Israel to the United States) shared how he had a routine of buying an Israeli newspaper every weekend from a tobacco store at the corner when he just moved to the United States several decades ago. But, things have dramatically changed with the plethora of digital newspapers:

> I'd read the *Ha'artetz* [elite Israeli newspaper] and Ynet [popular Israeli digital news source], you know, just for different perspectives, every morning, and then I check the *New York Times* and *Washington Post* here. But I find that, yeah, I do know more. I mean, I always find it interesting that, in terms of citizenship, those of us who came from the outside—and maybe because we had to take a citizenship test—actually know more about politics here and about government, and, you know, I have to teach my students about how legislation is

being passed in Congress, so I'm an expert on American politics and American policy by virtue of my own interest. And so forth. And, so I definitely stay connected; I think it's really important.

Homeland news consumption seems to change over time, becoming less comprehensive and more selective. Daily news of personal political clashes, local economic fluctuation, individual crime stories, among others, seem to lose value, with individual tastes and interests taking their place. For example, Constantinos (Greek to the United States) explained,

> I think it really depends on the issue. So, if something happened in Greece that would affect my mom's pension or health, from a political perspective, that would make me very upset. Or something that would jeopardize the Greek standing in the world, let's say. Right, so that would definitely make me very upset. Here, again, it depends on what would be the effect. Right? If it's something that's affecting my daughter, right, something about her education, for example. That would likely make me more upset than, they changed the tax law.

Major events or crises awaken a great interest in news from the homeland, as related by Anna (Cyprus/Greece to the United Kingdom):

> I do [consume news] when there's a crisis. Or a big event. So, when the leftist party came to power in Greece, that was a big thing for me. And I followed that very closely. When there's a big crisis in Cyprus, there is now something—a big news story that happened there that I'm following. I have to say, I'm surprising myself by having very little interest in the political debates in Cyprus. So, I was more interested in a story that had to do with migration in Cyprus rather than the crisis, you know, that has to do with the divide of the country.

Gradual disengagement from news seems to take place over time and reflects a more general transition in orientation toward the world and one's place in it. Lynn (the United States to Europe) vocalized the process that she went through:

I don't read U.S. papers anymore, necessarily. I just read the world news. Because I find myself, as I'm living in Europe, I'm also trying to understand the European system. The European elections were yesterday, and for me, that's a—although I can't vote because I'm not European—I want to be informed, I want to understand. And so, I'm far more aware of the broader world in which I live, but also where my students come from. I teach in an international classroom. I play a very big role in a society that prides itself on internationalization. So, for me, that's been a clear effort. But, it was a—it was a very big learning curve to realize how American I was. And that's not bad, but it's certainly affected my teaching.

How relevant news is to one's personal life circumstances becomes, over time, a core motivation to keep up with it or less so. For example, Patrick (the United Kingdom to Belgium) explained,

> I've always had the capacity, in all the places I've lived, of thinking, OK, this is where I am. You get the stuff up on the internet, on the news page. On MSN stuff comes up, maybe you read it. But I don't seek it out, no. I know vaguely about Brexit. It will have some marginal effects on me, but I can become a Belgian citizen very quickly or a Swedish citizen because of my wife. So, it's not going to really affect my life.

Similarly, Claire (Canada to the United States) feels she can't make a difference anyway, so she is better off getting informed about U.S. politics:

> I just can't deal with any more of that. And I don't get to vote, so I'm sort of like, "Mmm, I can't change things." I pay much more attention to U.S. politics. Far, far more. Although I've kind of been throwing my hands up in the air about it lately, I watch, I watch the news almost every day. I read the *New York Times* and the *Post*, usually about ten stories collectively, every day, at a minimum. We talk about politics at home a lot.

From analyzing the discussion over the news, one gets a sense that often there was a blurring of the act of consuming news with actually being active and engaged: consuming news is perceived as a proxy for being involved and connected. This was particularly salient when one's home country experienced a crisis of sorts—whether natural or human-caused disaster, armed conflict, or major celebration of a big "win." During these times news consumption occupied significantly more time and attention in comparison to routine days. Clearly, this became the case for me with the events of October 7, 2023, and the violence on both sides that broke out. I found myself refreshing my news sources constantly, desperate for some good news, dreading seeing another name of someone familiar and another image of devastation and humanitarian disasters.

Media during COVID-19

COVID-19 created a unique challenge for immigrants, in addition to the existential threats and hardship that everyone else was experiencing. My account may be illuminating, as sheltering at home in New Jersey, one of the hotspots of the outbreak, rocked my boat in unexpected ways. While I always started the day checking an Israeli newspaper online, during the pandemic I did so obsessively, multiple times each day, checking every detail related to how COVID-19 affected my homeland; constantly comparing it with New Jersey (as both states are very similar in terms of population size and geography).

I started clinging to Israeli humor and memes forwarded to me on social networks by my family and friends (and, ever a researcher, analysis of this collection later became a research project with a close colleague).[6] There was something about the nuances of this humor that was so familiar, so comforting, so "homey" (unfortunately, Israel's history has included multiple opportunities to develop unique, particularly morbid forms of humor, mostly accessible "in the group").

Uncharacteristically, I read translated thrillers in Hebrew left behind by an Israeli relative during her visit last summer. Similarly, I ended an intense working-remotely day by watching an Israeli soap opera on Netflix. Neither genre is my cup of tea, but at the time immersing myself in my native language of Hebrew became a source of security, strength, and comfort. Needless to say, connecting with my siblings and their families as well as elderly relatives and extended family members in Israel, which we did regularly B.C. [before COVID] as well, added another layer of meaning, depth, emotion, and urgency.

At the same time, I was clinging excitedly to every piece of news that highlighted the Israeli health system's approach to mitigating COVID-19 as a potential role model for doing things better than they were handled in the United States, feeling a deep sense of pride.

Being an immigrant during COVID-19, as will be discussed further in chapter 8, had unique layers of meaning, but it also serves me here to highlight how media may take on additional roles for immigrants during a crisis. To the traditional roles served by media at a time of crisis—such as providing information, interpretation, and escapism—we can add, when it comes to immigrants, a very central role of a bridge to their homeland.[7] "Digital kinship" (e.g., keeping an eye on each other and maintaining intimacy at a distance) was manifest particularly through immigrants' heightened sense of responsibility for care of their elderly parents back home during the pandemic via technological mediation.[8]

Finally, COVID-19 also brought out more forcefully the fact that digitalization is not only used for sustaining a sense of community but is also used for surveillance and control of borders in the concrete territorial sense.[9] With the many practices of biometric and visualization technologies, for example, migrants become not only connected via digitalization processes but also screened and controlled.[10]

"Imaginary Homeland"

Food, native language, media, maintaining cultural traditions, returning home for visits, and socializing with expats were all strategies employed by the participants in my study to nourish their identities[11] At the same time, most of them also emphasized that they are investing in adjusting and familiarizing themselves with the culture of their new homes, especially as they interact with students and colleagues in the institution of higher education and as they raise their children intentionally to hold hybrid identities. Many of them invoked the need to navigate multiple cultures and used all forms of media available to them to construct for themselves a sense of belonging. They were aware of the struggles and need for constant negotiations between their homeland culture and their new home culture. Indeed, they seem to acknowledge their hybrid and fluid cultural existence in a "Third Space" without naming it as such.[12] While challenged by the complexity of their situation, they also believed that they had a richer sense of being in an increasingly globalized world.

At the end of a very insightful interview, when discussing the various ways by which she sustains and challenges her Indian identity in the diaspora, and her parental approach to her children's dual identity, Anamika (India to the United States) said, "Salman Rushdie says that people living here, the Indian community, you know, they create what is called 'Indias of the mind.'"[13] "Indias of the mind" evokes the sense of loss that diasporic communities feel and their need to acknowledge that it is impossible to reclaim that past from afar, thus creating fictions in their minds about their homeland that don't really exist as such. The theme of loss that cannot be reclaimed surfaced in the interviews when talking with the participants about the possibility of a "return" home. This is the topic of the next chapter.

8

The Return

Would They Consider Going Back?

"Better to Just Have Them in Memory"

I am often asked, "Will you ever go back to Israel?" "Will you return?" The answer is probably a "No," but it is much easier to respond, "I don't think so." It is less definite. It is easier to swallow. It is easier to live with. Our three grown-up children have made lives for themselves in North America. They have partners; they have children. I cannot imagine not being a drive away from them. But what about my siblings in Israel with whom I am very attached? We are all aging... Will we be able to continue to visit each other? COVID-19 reminded us how tangible this privilege is... What about my nieces and nephews and their children, my cousins, my friends, my former Ph.D. students? Will I remain part of their lives? Will they be part of mine?

And what about aging and dying, and wishes for burial? There is not a piece of land in the United States where I feel I belong enough to wish to be buried there. Can it be California, where my husband is from? Ohio, where I went for graduate school and had my first two children? Kansas, where I completed my post-doc? Pennsylvania, where I was on a scholarship for a semester? Washington state, where I spent a sabbatical? Illinois, where my first position in the United

States took place? New Jersey, where I am now? New York, where our older son lives? Massachusetts, where our young daughter lives? Or perhaps even Toronto, Canada, where our middle son lives? If anywhere in the world, it has to be in my home country, Israel. I probably would have loved to be buried in the graveyard in my sister's kibbutz in the northern part of the country. It is a beautiful spot, so serene, among olive trees overlooking picturesque hilly fields. When spring comes, it is dotted with pink cyclamens and red anemones peeking from between the rocks. My beloved mother is buried there. My sister's family will probably be as well, when the time comes. It could have been comforting to think of such an option. But what would it mean for my children to have to worry and maintain a grave from across the ocean, and to feel an obligation to spend limited resources of money and time to go back to the gravesite for an annual memorial event? I can't really do that to them knowingly. So, we resorted to cremation, which makes the most sense for many reasons. I told them, "Do spread my ashes in the Atlantic Ocean—so they symbolize the fluid travel between my two home countries, Israel and the United States, flowing back and forth with the waves."

Since this issue was weighing heavily on my mind, I asked these questions of my interviewees as well: "Will you go back?" "Where do you wish to end your life?" "What are your wishes for handling your body after death?" Questions that we are not often asked directly but that are often on our minds. I was positively surprised: rather than being offended, caught off guard, or embarrassed, they were eager to answer and share their internal deliberations. I just had to ask them.

Like me, the most common answer was, probably not returning to the homeland. There is really not much left to return to, besides nostalgia and memories. Parents are, or will be, deceased; the house where I grew up has long been sold, demolished, or renovated; friends and family members have moved away; and the country has changed. It does not feel like home anymore. As we discussed in chapter 7, the "imaginary homeland" created via engagement with various cultural forms from the Diaspora cannot be reclaimed in practice, and often the physical visit back home reveals the gap between the imaginary and the real.[1] "Psychologically, I've totally left" is how Patrick (Scotland to Belgium) captured it so succinctly. Mayur (India to the United States) elaborated:

> As years go by, I feel like I get more and more disconnected. [...]
> Any time I've gone back to India, I've found it much more changed
> than the last time I saw it. [...] So that's why with the passing years
> I feel more and more disconnected from India. Also, my main
> connection there is my mom. [...] Sure, I'll have nostalgia and
> I would want to visit; I would want to take my kids there to show
> them, you know. But I'm not sure that those places would even exist,
> where I grew up. And I often have this kind of almost a fear that
> I would go back and I would regret, actually, that it's all gone. You
> know. [...] It's better to just have them in memory and think that
> maybe they still exist, those places still exist, and they haven't
> changed or whatever. But it's almost like I don't want to take the
> chance of actually going to those places and finding out, oh my god,
> what happened.

Similarly, Tamir (Israel to the United States) was also reflecting on what probably does not exist anymore: "You know, you build your social life here, have friends here. And there is, in many ways—that's my kind of theory—that when you imagine going back to your old country, what you have in mind is what you left. Not what you're coming to now. And when I was thinking of returning then, it was not tempting.

The sense of loss that is embedded in many of the answers is softened by an expression of acceptance. "I don't envision going back to Argentina," said Jose (Argentina to the United States):

> I don't know what would have to happen in my life for me to make
> that decision. But it's not my plan. No, I don't see it now. We are
> happy here; we don't want to go anywhere. [...] I came to terms with
> the idea that I would never come to terms, because (a) I don't want to
> be frustrated with this sort of gap that I still feel, and second, ... I
> hate whining. ... If there is something that you don't like, you find a
> way to solve it. I mean, accept it as is; that's the way things are. Come
> to terms with it. And that's, you know, the way that it is.

The way it is, according to Jose and many others, is that going back is not an option. Similarly, Mina (India to the United States) was reflecting,

I feel like my main connection to home now is to my parents, and I feel like once they pass away, I don't know if I will have that base. You know? Of course, India will still be my home. [...] I don't envision any time when I am married that I'm going to be able to go back home because it's become clear that's what I have sort of—what I have compromised. And I'm fine with that because I have a wonderful partner, and you know, I'm grateful for that. So, maybe if I'm widowed, I might consider going back to India, but I don't know. It depends on how India will be at that time.

Others were playing with the idea of retiring into a split life—going back and forth from their current home to their home of origin, enjoying both the present and the past, and building on what they can offer them to complement each other. Cosmas (Nigeria to the United States) shared his hopes: "My ideal situation would be going back to Africa, coming back here. So I'll have my home here as well as, you know, us going crisscrossing [...] that's my idea. Maybe during wintertime, you say, 'OK, you can deal with your winter. I'm going back to Nigeria.'"

Juan (Mexico to the United States) was starting to play with a fantasy of his: "There is a small possibility... my wife loves Mexico, so we had talked about the possibility of being in both Canada and Mexico at different times. I had fantasized about having a retirement home in Mexico [...] that I'd live part of the year there.... It's though we are getting older, and we should start thinking more seriously about these issues."

Similarly, Alisha (India to the United States) shared, "After retirement, we are hoping that we can, you know, be in India for a few months, and also live here in the U.S., wherever we are [...] and it also depends on the children's requirements, right? If they—wherever they are, and they need any help. [...] But maybe after we retire, we'll spend more time in India, and you know, we'll be back and forth between India and the U.S." Smita (India to the United States] added another motivation for a split residency type of life: "I have not given back in a way... I have not done nearly what I could do. [...] I would do more back-and-forth."

Of the 3Ps that offered explanations for immigrating in the first place—personal, professional, and political, only two, the personal and political, surfaced once again in the discussion of the possibility of going back to the homeland. At this point in people's advanced lives and careers, professional opportunities seemed rare at the horizon and less relevant for the senior and aging phases of one's academic journey. This stage of immigration life is different from the early days, when one just explores the possibility of relocation via a temporary position like a post-doc appointment. According to a study of Israelis, for example, who returned to Israel after such short-term experiences in the United States, they felt a sense of alienation and missed the social support despite the comforts afforded them by the American lifestyle. They were too attached to their social networks of family and friends in Israel, to the Hebrew language and cultural and geographical landscapes, and have chosen to return and settle for a much less desired position and significantly reduced materialistic rewards.[2] Time away from the original home and strong identity attachments thus seem to play a major role in the decision to return.

Personal Considerations

Children weigh heavily in the realization that going back to their country of origin is not often a realistic option for many. Wherever the children are located will probably determine retirement location. Constantinos (Greece to the United States) expressed it in this way: "I can see ourselves going back to Greece for retirement. [...] But it all depends on where my daughter is, right? If she's in Spain or London, you know, it will be easier for us to be in Greece than on the East Coast. So something to reflect over."

Jennifer (the United Kingdom to the United States) was even more specific about the central role of children in retirement decisions: "My life is here. My kids, right now are here, and certainly, you know, I'm at a point where a lot of our friends are thinking about retirement, and obviously, we're thinking... People talk about where they'll move for retirement. We say we'll move near to our most attentive children. Whoever's most attentive, that's where we'll move."

While for many academics their children's choices are restricting their options, for others, they feel like providing opportunities. Jozef (Belgium to the United States) said, "A lot is riding on what happens to my children. What about college? What are their decisions going to be? If any of them ends up having children in the United States, and those kids are American, that's going to change the whole discussion as well. So, I really don't know. But I don't care, I feel, I mean, I think I've always been a little bit of a wanderer."

While children are a vector pulling the interviewees in one direction, mostly away from their homeland, elderly parents and siblings are pulling in the opposite direction, creating a difficult tension for many. Richard (Australia to the United States) shared with me,

> I was down with my family for Christmas time. They're getting old, you know. My elder sister is eighty-five, eighty-six. And their life is not necessarily easy. They're wonderful, wonderful people. And I kind of think, you know, what is my responsibility as a family member? I don't know, and I'll just see how things pan out with all of that. But, you know, where is home?

A close relationship with a sister is also the determining force for Lilian (Canada to the United States):

> The two major variables would be my sister and my family [. . .] even though my husband and I made all these lists of priorities, and we are trying to be very organized, emotionally, like, having my sister close by is so important to me as a person, as a sense of connection, having some support or giving support. Being needed, also, is so important to me that I think it would trump everything else, actually.

Many of the interviewees still had aging parents whom they hoped to still be in their lives upon retirement. Deep care for them and a sense of obligation were dominant in their thinking about moving back to be closer to them. "Hopefully my parents will be around much longer," said Nadya (Bulgaria to the United States), "and this is the one thing that is really, really stressing me out and worrying me, that as they grow older, knowing that if something happens at the very best of times, it would take me a couple of days to get there. As they grow older, it is pretty stressful." This sentiment resonated very strongly with me, as I moved in the United States from one position to another (among other reasons) to be closer to an international airport that would cut my travel time to Israel significantly, as my mother was aging and the anxiety over the day "*the phone call*" arrives was mounting.

The determination to go back home to take care of elderly parents was particularly apparent in Asian cultures. For example, Rhi Won (South Korea to the United States) put it in very clear terms:

> This is not about my future, but actually my dream. As I see my parents get old, I want to support them physically and financially and become their child who takes care of them. So we talk about this issue all the time and we fully agree on supporting each other's parents whenever they need us. [...] No matter what we have here—what kind of job, what status we are in—we will go back to support them if they need us.

Emma (China to the United States) clearly explained the cultural expectation: "I think as we grow older and our parents age, it also depends on their health conditions. 'Cause, especially for my parents-in-law, who only have my husband as their only son. And in China, they retire early. In China, it is the philosophy or the cultural thing that you should take care of your parents when they get old."

Rarer, but yet present, was a plan to go back home for a support system around a spouse's serious illness. Such was the case shared by Lynn (the United States to tEurope):

> There's the unspoken idea of family support. [...] The notion of whether you're going through a chronic disease or starting a family or having a family as an expat, I think, is uniquely challenging. Because the idea of, like if [your husband] is ill, and he's in the hospital or something, it's nice to have someone else who can come to the hospital and help out. It's not even nice just for him, but also, it's nice for me, in a very selfish way, just to say, like "I get an hour off to take a shower or something."

Relationships with siblings, parents, children, and spouses thus impact the thinking about future relocations, whether to justify staying put or to contemplate the possibility of going back.

Political Considerations

Similar to personal considerations, political considerations also served as both push and pull forces. My interviews were conducted under the shadow of the first Trump era in the United States and the threat of Brexit in the United Kingdom, and both emerged as meaningful considerations for and against relocation. Academics contemplated leaving the United States and the United Kingdom or were discouraged about the possibility of moving back to the United States or the United Kingdom because of these political waves. Such, for example, was the case of Claire (Canada to the United States), who confessed, "We have emergency plans to go back if bad things happen in America. So, when Trump came into office, we discussed alternatives."

Nathan (Israel to the United States) reflected,

> Politically, it's a nightmare in both countries, so, I don't see, you know, like, before Trump, people were saying, "Oh, you Israelis" and stuff. And now after Trump was elected, I'm saying, "You see? You can be a citizen of a country and not agree with your government." So, politically, it's not the best place to be. But I do see the advantages too. [...] I don't see it [going back to Israel] really happening. But it's an option that I have in my mind that it's something that might happen eventually, whatever circumstances might lead to it.

Brexit came up in the conversations with several of the interviewees as well. Lara (the United States to the United Kingdom) said, "I moved to London because of that city. It's a kind of cosmopolitan, multicultural, vibrant energy. And, so, if Brexit goes through on October 31st, you know, that would be very telling for me, about whether or not I stay. I don't have much of an interest in staying in the U.K. if it's not part of the EU."

And Anne (Canada to the United Kingdom) shared,

> We actually talked about this, especially since Boris Johnson became prime minister, and he seems to be heading—taking us down a no-deal route. And it's just becoming quite frightening, really. And we've just kind of said to each other, "Do we actually really want to stick around for this?" It feels like quite a tough position to be in because it does feel like things are closing in on us. We've just kind of joked around, saying, "Well, I guess it's time for a move—big move again."

Paula (Germany to the United Kingdom) was reflecting on similar issues:

With Brexit, we had to think a lot about this [applying for British citizenship] because we have a lot of colleagues, especially from those countries which are not as economically strong as Germany, and where people are really worried about their jobs. They've taken on British citizenship. And we decided that we didn't want to do this. I actually feel more German than I ever have, but still also European. One of the reasons, apart from our parents, why we wanted to actually sell our house in London was we were really upset. We feel European, and we were both so upset by Britain wanting to leave Europe that we also felt that, okay, in that case, you know, we don't really want to be here anymore. [...] The feelings were quite strong. Of feeling—being rejected as Europeans. And, even though London is a bubble, it's a cosmopolitan city, it still felt like "Hmmm, you know, I don't necessarily really want to be in this country anymore."

Political and social issues were at the heart of many other participants—from a variety of countries and over a multiplicity of concerns. For example, the political turmoil in Brazil at the time, with the rise of Bolsonaro's autocracy, appeared in all of the chats with interviewees originating in that country. For example, Eva (Brazil to Sweden) shared, "We did think about going back to Brazil, to spend some time there, but now, with the political situation, no. At the moment, no."

Cristina (Brazil to Portugal) responded to my question about moving back by saying, "It's really difficult to give a straight answer to this question because I'm really upset with the situation in Brazil right now. [...] So I don't know if this feeling I have now will last. It's like a relationship when you are mad at your partner. I'm mad at Brazil right now. So, I cannot think of going back."

Other countries also posed challenges for my interviewees who enjoyed the freedoms provided to them in the United States. For example, Gaus (Pakistan to the United States) said, "Because there is so much politically going on in Pakistan, I don't see any possibility [of going back]. So, for me, here, there is security and like, a freedom of speech. You get academic freedom here. Those are important things."

Others lamented at feeling alienated, and even depressed, about the situation in their home country. Mina (India to the United States) shared, sadly, "I don't have that sense of wanting to go back because when I do go back, sometimes I feel I'm a misfit in India. [...] So, it depends on how things are politically because I do not want to be in a place where I feel like my political values are not in line with where I am at." Hassan (Iran to the United States) recalled in great pain, "I am planning to after I retire, probably before I die, to go back. . . . But one trip I made home, I know, when I came back I got really depressed. [. . .] I'm afraid of going back to Iran. Afraid for my health, for my mental health. I don't talk about it."

Concerns over cultural shifts were brought up even in Western societies that seemed less prone to experience major political turmoil. For example, Lynn (the United States to Europe) was preoccupied with the changes in European attitudes toward "others": "I think, right now, my big factor is also how comfortable I feel. The foreigner—the anti-foreigner sentiment has been tough on me recently."

A few of the interviewees considered financial and/or employment constraints in moving back to their homeland. For example, Dick (Europe to Singapore) said, "There is a mandatory retirement at the age of sixty-seven, so then it is back to Norway." Amanda (the United Kingdom to the United States) reflected on her and her husband's deliberation about returning to the United Kingdom: "It's partly a financial decision, paying taxes on retirement funds in the U.K. if [they are] brought to the U.S. [. . .] and the other thing is health care—there is free health care in the U.K. for citizens. [. . .] So, you know, I think those kinds of financial considerations will affect whether we decide to stay or go back."

Similarly, guaranteeing good retirement support is what Andres (Norway to the United States) has in mind: "Norway is a very organized society. The U.S., at the moment, is increasingly fragmented. I could be completely wrong, but I don't count on my retirement necessarily providing the services that I need in the U.S., so I keep Norway as just a kind of safety valve if I need it. But I'm not particularly interested in going there."

The homeland as a default option, "just in case," seemed to be on the mind of quite a few of the academic immigrants in my study. Mina (India to the United States) offered a thoughtful analysis of her political concerns, which I relay here in detail:

> The politics of India have become too much. I feel it's—the India I grew up in was a very secular, religiously pluralistic place. And something has completely, terribly changed, and the way I see it, it's

becoming much, much more fascist. [...] So, but I still feel, in the U.S., that there is some resistance, and there is some hope, and there are some checks and balances. In India, though it's a democracy, the democracy has fully watered in a way... Like, supporting very, very hateful rhetoric. [...]

But also, I feel like raising a child—it's a hard decision. Like, sometimes I wonder, "Why am I raising a child in the south of the U.S.?" It's hard—given the politics there. But raising a child in India is also hard in a different way. Culturally, yeah, he would gain so much. But I think it's still—I don't know. So, I've kind of come to terms with the fact that I'm going to be in the U.S. And, because my husband, you know, he doesn't study these things and he's in a field where he doesn't see a lot of the racism or the sexism that I see and experience. So, I feel like his experience is very different. Like, how he sees the world is different.

And, so, but if I look at sexism, it's—I feel like I'm safer in the U.S. In India, I have to physically worry every time I go out to, you know, what path I'm going to take or what clothes I'm going to wear. That is not something I worry about daily here. That's huge. You know, so, in some instances, although I love my country and I have a lot that I've learned from it and owe so much back to it, now I've come to terms with the fact that being in the U.S., as an academic, gives me the voice to talk back to India in a way that I could not have done in India.

And I'm afraid, what would have become of me if I stayed back in India? Because I would have been shaped by the same kind of politics that would have probably made me also become like some of my friends and family are now. [...] Like, there's only the ultraconservative. And if you're not that, you're not considered Hindu, or not considered Indian. Which is antithetical to what it means to be Indian. It's actually to be open to different religions.

And that's what is Gandhi's India that I was raised in. Today, Gandhi has become a negative figure. An evil figure. Gandhi was assassinated by a Hindu nationalist. The Hindu nationalists are in power today. They are celebrating. There is a temple for the assassin of Gandhi. And they're digging up all kind of dirty laundry about Gandhi and making him, like, the bad guy who forced India to be secular. Otherwise, we would have been a Hindi nation. I mean, this is ridiculous.

End-of-Life Considerations

Finally, considerations about dying came up in the conversations quite openly and rationally. For Evan (Belgium to Europe), it determined his choice of location:

> Belgium is still a Catholic country to some degree. Catholics would deny the right to choose the moment of your death. But my university has been one of the main proponents, and actually activists in euthanasia legislation and I feel quite strongly about that. Yes, it's a matter of having that choice. It's not a matter of using the choice, even, but it's a matter of having that opportunity to decide on your life and yourself. [...] I wouldn't mind dying in countries where there is legislation concerning euthanasia.

Dying in a place that feels more like home, and close to family, seemed to emerge as a priority. Violeta (Chile to the United States) said,

> When I'm thinking about, you know, retiring to Spain, I was thinking I would live maybe half the year there, but really be half the year here, because this is where my children are. And I want to be close to them. [...] When we talk about going to Spain, it gets me—to eventually think—I will come back here, you know, to die.

As in my own case, one's children seem to be a major concern for many other participants as well: "Buried? I don't give a damn," said Eddy (Europe to Israel). "It's really my kids. I don't want them—they are not interested in praying on a grave, so, ashes to ashes, that's it." For others, their religious belief frees them from the desire to be buried, as Mina (India to the United States) expressed: "Some people have this strong thing that they need to be buried in their homeland and things like that. I don't have—as a Hindu, I'm going to be burned into ashes, so it doesn't matter. It will all go back to the earth."

Anamika (India to the United States) shared with me in detail how her line of thinking about dying has evolved. She related the following:

> I always felt like I couldn't die in the U.S. Like, death would not happen here. Almost like I was immortal because, how can death

happen in the United States because this is not my place? It was this kind of surreal feeling that I had. I realized at one point. "What are you thinking? This is so illogical." [...]

So, it was a very strange thing I went through, you know, about ten years into being here. Then I realized, "Whoa, you're not immortal just because you're here. You can die any time, and it could be on this soil." So first, my heart is partly there. So, what would I do? I would do it like my Dad; it would be cremation. Cremation, of course, is normal for Indians. So that's not unusual, right? It's normal. But I would not have them take my ashes to India. I would have them scatter them where they felt appropriate because I would want them to do it where they feel a connection. [...]. I would like them to be scattered in the water because that's our tradition, that the ashes should be put in the water because then we're set free."

In reflecting on the accounts of most of my interviewees, I learn that they accept their double lives as a constant, not only while living but also in projecting the end of life. Like other immigrants, their longing for the past is part of who they are, a bittersweet situation that defines them at the core. Those who have children believe that they will be freed from such complexity and will have a strong core identity and sense of home. At the same time, they also hope for them to maintain some cultural ties to their parents' homeland—not so much as a residential option, but as an enrichment of their sense of self.

9

The Support

What Can Be Done to Help
Academic Immigrants?

"It's Personal for Me"

In reviewing the hundreds of transcript pages from the eighty-one interviewees, I was struck by the richness of their narratives. It was quite a challenge to choose just a few relevant quotes and yet for them to serve as representative exemplars of the themes that emerged during the analysis. There is so much there. This book does not do full justice to the many additional aspects of this exploration and the nuances of difference: gender, culture, location, institution, seniority, personality, personal circumstances, and the like. I was only able to paint some of the issues with broad brush strokes, prioritizing the voices of interviewees over my interpretation and analysis.

I also reflected on how many interviewees I knew beforehand (even if very superficially). It caused me to wonder whether over the years of international networking, I somehow gravitated toward other immigrants—and that it was not just coincidental. Many interviewees also shared that they bonded with other immigrants, not necessarily from the same background, feeling a sense of solidarity in similar experiences and sensibilities. More specifically, about my personal reflections, what may seem strange to some, I found comradeship with Arab colleagues from our home region, seemingly on the "other side of the divide," as we bonded via our concerns, fears, and critiques of "The Conflict." Looking at my homeland from a distance—geographically as well as mentally—seemed to have closed the gaps between us to focus on the commonalities and humanity, rather than on our ongoing brutal conflict. A former Palestinian student whose parents were refugees of the Nakba (the Arabic term for the Palestinian "catastrophe" resulting from Israel's war of independence) always signs his emails to me with Salaam/Shalom (peace in Arabic and Hebrew). We humorously call each other "cousin" (following the biblical telling of the familial relationship between Jews and Arabs). When former President Trump announced the Muslim ban, I sent him a note of support. He sent me a note of comfort and prayers after the Tree of Life synagogue shooting in Pittsburg. Since October 7, 2023, we have been corresponding periodically to share our grief and hopes.

Finally, when I consider the contributions of our academic immigrant colleagues, I am also reflecting on my career-long efforts to advocate for the study of populations and issues that are not necessarily WEIRD-focused (Western, Educated, Industrialized, Rich, Democratic).[1] A large portion of our research in my immediate and related field of children and media leaves much to be desired in terms of relevancy to broad parts of the globe. Nevertheless, there is an assumption of universality. Studies from countries outside the Western world—and notably outside the United States—are "case studies," and authors are reluctant to put the name of the country in the title because of concern over lower citation rates. At the same time, U.S.-based research is largely perceived as universal.[2] As scholars, we are embedded in our societies and institutions, and we study the familiar and the accessible. It also means that we may be unfamiliar even with the ways our implicit biases shape the questions we ask, as we do not know what we do not know.

I am very much aware that in the contemporary political moment of the strengthening of nationalistic movements in many parts of the world, the challenges to internationalizing the academy are many. This reality is conflated in schools and departments of communication, media, and journalism, where the majority of my interviewees are employed, with the dramatic developments in our disciplines, the eroding trust of the public in the news media, and the pervasive dissemination of disinformation and misinformation. We are witnessing the consequences in the academy as well, providing a fertile ground for silencing nonconventional voices, strangling differences, and marginalizing otherness. As I argued in chapter 5, I believe that the academic immigrants among us, the "outsiders," infuse our work with different ways of thinking, asking questions, and doing research. They challenge us to reveal our implicit biases and preferences. They enrich our personal lives. They contribute to making us better scholars, and better humans.

In an era where issues of diversity, equity, and inclusion are so prominent in the mission of higher education as it struggles with the growing counterpressure from conservative political forces around the world, it is also valuable to highlight that academic immigrants seem to be much more open to embracing values of inclusiveness and equity in all aspects of their academic life. As Mayur (India to the United States) explained,

> Issues like diversity and inclusion are more personal to me. It's not something that I just learned because somebody said we should care about this. You know, it's something that I had to kind of work with throughout, as long as I've been in this country coming from India. Because it wasn't always given. It was something that at times you had to kind of fight for, and sometimes you had to kind of make a case for. I'm sympathetic to people who are immigrants, whether they are in academia or not because I've seen that struggle.

Thus, in addition to contributing to research and student learning, academic immigrants also help to achieve institutional goals related to diversity and equity.

Despite these contributions, the composite portrait shared by academic immigrants who participated in my study is complicated: while not overtly discriminated against in their institutions, they feel they are not fully included. Many continue to feel like outsiders, at least to some degree, even after decades of holding academic positions in institutions of higher education. Most of the academic immigrants I interviewed live full and rich lives, enjoy flourishing careers, and are most grateful for the opportunities afforded to them. While experiencing many challenges, their struggles are less acute in comparison to those of many academics from the global south who attempted to be integrated into European institutions of higher education, especially around gender and racial inequalities.[3] At the same time, they feel they are living a double life: they are tormented by accident or natural disasters back home, aging and ailing parents who are far away, and/or the political turmoil and conflicts they can only witness from a distance. The mental strain of being unable to be completely grounded in the "here and now" but living at the same time in the "there and then" is a constant challenge to their wellbeing. The COVID-19 pandemic exacerbated this situation, as suddenly travel to visit one's home country became impossible, and the future of travel previously taken for granted was now uncertain. This double-life state of mind, invisible and unaccounted for by the academic community, requires acknowledgment, understanding, and compassion.

For my part, as an academic immigrant professor and administrator, I contend that academic immigrants, scholars, and teachers who hold key positions in our academic institutions require significantly more appreciation for their contributions to all aspects of academic life, as well as much more recognition of and support for the unique challenges that they face. Offices of diversity and inclusion should address their needs specifically by, for example, celebrating the breadth of diverse nationalities among the academic workforce on their campus; helping to build and resource supportive peer networks (patterned after those designed for other minoritized faculty groups); addressing the issues and supports needed by academic immigrants in diversity training, policies, and outreach messaging; highlighting and celebrating the diverse holidays and cultural practices celebrated on campus by both students and faculty; and acknowledging major current events happening in faculty members' home countries (both major accomplishments as well as disasters).

Additionally, promotion and reappointment evaluations of such faculty should make limited use of standardized student evaluation surveys (known for being biased against women, people of color, nonbinary faculty, faculty with disabilities, and others, as discussed in chapter 3), supplementing these data points with additional evidence of effectiveness, such as peer teaching evaluations. In addition to acknowledging the contributions that these faculty members are making, such educational, policy, and resource initiatives can help connect international faculty with their compatriots, helping them become more integrated into their institutional community.

In my efforts to learn from my participants, I developed the following recommendations for institutions of higher education to help academic immigrants find more welcoming homes in our midst, where our differences are our strengths. It is certainly a partial list to stimulate interest and motivation to apply and add more.

We know all too well that the academe is a site of struggle. In this arena, conflicts are played out between bodies of knowledge, different power structures, and competing views about what the world is and how it should be, and individuals navigate their place within it throughout their academic trajectory.[4] The constant struggle for academic freedom and free speech that we are witnessing in the United States currently, as well as the assault on the values of diversity and inclusion, are a reminder that the struggles are constantly changing, adjusting, and negotiating. The pendulum of care for diversity and inclusion will probably continue to swing back and forth, but for those of us who are interested in supporting our immigrant colleagues, here are some ideas to start with:

1. Learn our names and try to pronounce them correctly.

    Names are central signals of identity and meaning. Many of us really care that you make the effort to respect ours, even if it takes time and practice. Do not be afraid to ask us to pronounce it for you or correct you. Such a sincere effort means a lot. Apologize and learn from your mistakes. Remember, your name may sound just as strange to us, and we are making an effort to learn it too.

2. Be patient with our linguistic skills and accents.

    Our English pronunciation may sound incomprehensible to you. We understand it makes communication difficult. Imagine how incomprehensible you sound to us. We are all learning to communicate. With time and practice, our interactions will become more fluent and more accessible. The more we talk to each other, the more practice we get, the better we will become. Don't avoid talking to us because it requires such effort.

3. Recognize and show an interest in our main cultural holidays.

    Many of us continue to celebrate the cultural and religious holidays of our country of origin. Knowing when our holidays occur is the first thing you can do in this regard. Investigate if your institution maintains an international holiday calendar; if not, propose that DEI administrators create one.

Also, you will find we have many fascinating customs and traditions; many are actually quite similar to your own. Ask about them. Hold international holiday events, exchange recipes, wish us a happy holiday, ask us about our plans and what we miss from our home country.

4 Show an interest in major current events happening in our home country.

Many of us live double lives in our former and present countries. We are joyful when a peace treaty has been signed at home. We burst with pride when a compatriot wins a Nobel Prize. But most of the time we are worried about a violent conflict, political turmoil, or natural disaster in our homeland. We probably have family and friends back there, so we are concerned and maintain constant communication with them. Ask us how they are doing.

Of course, geopolitical borders do not keep those worries away. We often start our day by scrolling our home news source on our phones before we check the local weather. If I am from India, express my condolences for a horrific accident. Turkey—ask me what I think about the results of recent elections. Eastern Europe—ask me if the war in Ukraine affects me personally. Syria—ask if I have relatives and friends who are refugees. Show sincere curiosity and empathy.

Help organize disciplinary-relevant academic events (e.g., "Western media's coverage of the uprising in Iran," in a School of Journalism with a member from Iran, or "Innovations in earthquake-resistance planning" in a School of Engineering with a member from Turkey).

More broadly, demonstrate in multiple ways that you understand we are all part of a global world of interconnections.

5 Appreciate the strengths we bring to our institution and discipline.

We often ask different questions in class, in our scholarship, and committee meetings because we have different experiences. As a result, we provide unexpected insights and examples and apply new approaches. All of this expands the world of students and colleagues alike. Our differences are our strengths; there is a lot we can learn from one another.

6   Appreciate the challenges we are facing.

It is not easy to relocate. Often, we feel longing, guilt, or worry. We are frustrated by being unable to express ourselves with the same ease, accuracy, and nuance as you do in your native language. We have "black holes" in understanding pop culture or in trivia games. We are often "othered" or left out. Our keeping quiet may be perceived as ignorance or complicity, or our speech as aggressive and inappropriate.

7   Help us network with other members of the community from our homeland.

Provide community-building opportunities for us to bond with others who experience the same life circumstances in our new country. This will enable us to support each other, provide advice, enjoy the relief of speaking in our native language and humor, support compatriot social events, and invite international guests to campus for us to enjoy and be proud of us.

Introduce international students to faculty from their region. Connecting faculty and international students offers an important layer of mentorship, advice, and support that benefits the integration and success of both.

8   Employ multiple forms of teaching evaluations in reviewing promotion cases.

Do not rely solely on quantitative student surveys (known for being biased against those perceived as "others," as is well documented for women, people of color, nonbinary faculty, faculty with disabilities, etc.). Peer observations of teaching, review of teaching materials and graded assignments, and out-of-class pedagogical initiatives will provide you with a much more robust understanding of what we bring to our teaching.

9   Engage in culturally aware mentorship with—and by— academic immigrants.[5]

Apply an approach to mentorship that is culturally sensitive and considers how one shows up in the world: How our identities, cultural beliefs, and worldviews influence the mentoring advice we provide, the practices we adopt, and the priorities we set. The approach highlights the need to be conscious of the assumptions, biases, past experiences, and stereotypes that we hold that may impact mentoring relationships.

It also encourages the adaptation of strategies that reduce and counteract such impacts and fosters trusting, culturally responsive relationships.

10 Expect your institution's Office of Diversity and Inclusion to include academic immigrants as part of their mandate.

DEI offices should address our immigrant members in ways patterned after those designed for other minoritized faculty groups in diversity training, policies, and outreach messaging. Some of us are people of color but not defined as "historically marginalized groups" (i.e., Afro-Americans, Latinx, and Native Americans), and some of us are not people of color at all. We are a heterogeneous group, just like gender or LGBTQ+ communities. All of us require the attention and resources of higher administration.

In practicing inclusive strategies, such as those presented here, we—collectively—hope that the common question we are regularly faced with, "Where are you from," will become an expression of your acknowledgment of our value and contribution to our institution, rather than one of peculiarity, oddity, strangeness, even uniqueness.[6]

Postscript

Once an Immigrant, Always an Immigrant

I was in the middle of writing this manuscript when the October 7, 2023, massacre on Israel shocked the world, and another Israel-Hamas round of violence erupted and is still raging as I write these final words. Suddenly, all I could do was refresh all the news sources on my phone every two minutes, live on WhatsApp exchanges with immediate family members and friends day and night, and engage in emotional eating (7 pounds in 4 weeks!). The rise of anti-Semitism on U.S. campuses, the silence of many campus leaders, the erasure of concern for Jewish life in top universities in the United States and the United Kingdom, and the show of indifference or helplessness from offices of Diversity, Equity, and Inclusion (DEI) who did not consider Jews a minority in need of protection was shocking at first and frightening later.

Suddenly the sense of our existence through double lives became overwhelming. The anxiety and confusion I was experiencing were embedded in a deep sense of loneliness and alienation from my networks of liberal-inclined colleagues, feminist sisterhood networks, and friends. Suddenly it did not matter that I have been a peace and feminist activist all my adult life, that I left Israel fourteen years ago, that I have strongly opposed the occupation and supported a two-state solution for Israel and the Palestinians for decades, that I have been critical of the current government and the rise of right-nationalism in Israel. Simply, I was Jewish and that was enough, in principle, to vilify someone like me in the eyes of the over-simplistic binary and conspiracy worldview as evil, colonialist, oppressor, genocidal that doesn't belong in mainstream society. Who I was as a person did not matter. I was reduced to a vilified category of Jews. Zionists, like my family and friends (people who believe in the right of Jews who have been persecuted for centuries for a homeland in their ancient land of Zion) were declared "not human." The institutions and people that were nourishing a sense of diasporic community—synagogues, restaurants owned by Israelis, Israeli speakers, artists, and performers—have become targets of boycotting, harassment, and threats. The sense of vulnerability and temporality that many immigrants and minoritized groups live with has grown exponentially deeper.

I found myself seeking and interacting more intensely with Jewish colleagues on campus and in my virtual networks, joining WhatsApp groups of Israelis on the East Coast of the United States, obsessively reading books and articles on anti-Semitism, and attending webinars and symposia. I tried to intellectually dissect anti-Semitism's roots on the White supremacy side on one hand and the radical left on the other hand, trying to understand how all of that could happen seemingly overnight (of course it has been simmering for centuries). I suddenly felt more Jewish than I ever felt before.

Amid this darkness, we were blessed with a gorgeous new granddaughter. However, the happiness she brought us was muddied with fear for her future—as a second-generation, Jewish-Israeli girl in a world that once again associates Jews with all the evils of the world. It was too much to bear. It still is.

Like many other Israelis in the Diaspora, we are experiencing a complete fragmentation of our identity as Israelis and as Jews, tormented by a moral breakdown, torn by guilt feelings for policies creating an unbearable humanitarian crisis in Gaza that we oppose and are not responsible for; traumatized by the intergenerational post-traumatic stress disorder of the Holocaust as the ground is shaking underneath us; experiencing deep grief, pain, and existential fear for our loved ones back in Israel; believing in the right of our people to have our only Jewish state and yet supporting the right of Palestinians for self-determination. Many of us are dealing with a shuttered sense of self and its relationship to Israel and to the world we live in, and searching for the renewed meaning of our Jewish identity that is aligned with our humane Jewish values.[1]

A lot of opinion pieces, commentaries, in-depth articles, and political and cultural analyses have already been written and will surely continue to be written about the domino effect of the October 7th massacre. I will not dwell on this topic here, except to say that the excruciating identity work that I was thrown into overnight has taught me one important lesson about this research project: once an immigrant, always an immigrant.

I will never be able not to be an immigrant. Neither will I want to, nor will I be allowed to be so. There are plenty of historical examples that speak to this conclusion (think of the Japanese camps in the United States during World War II or the hatred inflicted on Chinese people once COVID-19 hit as examples in the United States). But if I thought before that the academic world is different and if I assumed before that my privileged position as a distinguished university professor and a dean would protect me from that sense of alienation, I have sobered up overnight.

In one of the exchanges during our ongoing correspondence following October 7, 2023, after sharing with her an article about anti-Semitism on American campuses, Maya (Israel to the United Kingdom) wrote to me an email (February 19, 2024) that included the following text:[2]

> It is such a heavy heavy feeling; a mix of profound disappointment and disillusionment, unease, fear, anxiety, an imposed shame (as if we are Bibi's emissaries), and a sense of homelessness . . . not being wanted where we are (or frankly anywhere else in the world) but not wanting to return to where we came from either. There is something specific about academia that makes this particularly painful and upsetting, not just because we work in academia, but also because of what academia is supposed to embody.

What academia is supposed to embody is knowledge, truth, facts, historical context, rejection of conspiracy theories, ability to hold different conflicting truths at the same time, understanding nuance, engagement in open debate, an ability to express opposing opinions and views, and safety, both personal and collective. None of these have been extended to Israelis or Jews more generally following the war. Equating all Jews and all Israelis with all possible evils in the world—past and present—equating Judaism with Zionism and Zionism with fascism and perceiving Zionists as the last barrier to social justice in the world has been devastating to us. The allies we marched with hand-in-hand—during the Civil Rights movement, the Black Lives Matter movement, the feminist movement, the Take Back the Night movement, the labor movement, the climate change movement, and the LGBTQ+ movement—they all turned their back overnight to Jews, seemingly collectively. The sense of betrayal and shock became unbearable.

I have never been personally attacked or even threatened (at least until this moment in time). In my university, anti-Semitic and Islamophobic incidences have been mostly under control, and the higher administration has demonstrated concern to keep it this way. I have no idea what my colleagues are saying on social media, in their classrooms, in the petitions they sign, and at demonstrations, but they are respectful and kind toward me. I hope it is not only because I am in a position of power over them. But despite it all, it is the concept of "me" that has been deeply shuttered. It feels existential.

My postscript is left open-ended, as we don't know what tomorrow will bring. Will there be an end to the war atrocities for both sides? Will the world reconfirm the right of Israel to exist? Will Israel recognize the right of the Palestinians to self-determination? Will anti-Semitism be contained or grow? Will I find a Third Space where I will feel comfortable, safe, affirmed, "at home?"

This is what is on my mind right now, but I am not unique. Different academic immigrants experience the occasional crisis that reminds them that "once an immigrant, always an immigrant" and that belonging is fluid and is always a work in progress.

I cannot end this book without a note of hope. Raised in the Jewish tradition of Tikkun Olam (translated from Hebrew as "repairing the world"), according to which humans are collectively responsible for repairing the world made unjust by them, I am drawn to this quote as a vision for the future:

> Beloved community is formed not by the eradication of difference but by its affirmation, by each of us claiming the identities and cultural legacies that shape who we are and how we live in the world.
>
> —bell hooks[3]

Notes

Chapter 1 The Journey

1. Valdivia, A. (1999). A guided tour through one adolescent girl's culture. In S. R. Mazzarella & N. O. Pecora (Eds.), *Growing up girls: Popular culture and the construction of identity* (pp. 159–171). Peter Lang.
2. Gelman, A. (June 27, 2023). "How Academic Fraudsters Get Away with It." *Chronicle of Higher Education.* https://www.chronicle.com/article/how-academic-fraudsters-get-away-with-it
3. Lemish, D. (1987). Viewers in diapers: The early development of television viewing. In T. Lindlof (Ed.), *Natural audiences: Qualitative research of media uses and effects* (pp. 33–57). Ablex; Lemish, D., & Rice, M. L. (1986). Television as a talking picture book: A prop for language acquisition. *Journal of Child Language, 13,* 251–274.
4. Lemish, D. (1998). What is news? A cross cultural examination of kindergartners' understanding of news. *Communications: European Journal of Communication Research, 23,* 491–450; Lemish, D. (1997). Kindergartners' understandings of television: A cross cultural comparison. *Communication Studies, 48*(2), 109–126.
5. Lemish, D. (1998). Spice Girls' talk: A case study in the development of gendered identity. In S. A. Inness (Ed.), *Millennium girls: Today's girls around the world* (pp. 145–167). Rowman and Littlefield; Lemish, D. (2003). Spice World: Constructing femininity the popular way. *Popular Music and Society, 26*(1), 17–29; Nimrod, G., Elias, N., & Lemish, D. (2019). Grandparenting with media: Styles of mediating grandchildren's media use. *Journal of Family Studies, 28*(1), 70–88.
6. Nimrod, G., Elias, N., & Lemish, D. (2023). Like grandmother, like mother? Multi-generational mediation of young children's media use. *The International Journal of Communication, 17,* 4079–4096; Nimrod, G., Lemish, D., & Elias, N. (2020). Mediating grannies: Caring for young grandchildren's digital media use. *Essachess: Journal for Communication Studies,* special issue on aging and digital communication. Guest editors: L. Ivan, & A. Duduciuc. *13*(2), 41–58; Nimrod, G.,

Elias, N., & Lemish, D. (2019). Grandparenting with media: Styles of mediating grandchildren's media use. *Journal of Family Studies, 28*(1), 70–88.
7   hooks, b. (1991). Theory as liberatory practice. *Yale Journal of Law and Feminism, 4*, 1–12.
8   Lemish, D. (2010). *Screening gender in children's TV: The views of producers around the world.* Routledge.
9   Lemish, D. (Ed.). (2022). *The Routledge international handbook of children, adolescents and media* (rev. 2nd ed.). Routledge; Park, J., & Lemish, D. (2019). *KakaoTalk and Facebook: Korean American youth constructing hybrid identities.* Peter Lang; Götz, M., Lemish, D., & Holler, A. (2019). *Fear in front of the screen: Children's fears, nightmares and thrills.* Rowman & Littlefield; Lemish, D., & Götz, M. (Eds.). (2017). *Beyond the stereotypes? Boys, girls, and their images.* The International Clearinghouse of Children, Youth and Media, University of Gothenburg, Sweden, Nordicom; Lemish, D., Jordan, A., & Rideout, V. (Eds.). (2017). *Children, adolescents and media: The future of research and action.* Routledge; Lemish, D. (2015). *Children and media: A global perspective.* Wiley-Blackwell; Lemish, D. (Ed.). (2013). *The Routledge international handbook of children, adolescents and media.* Routledge; Götz, M., & Lemish, D. (Eds.). (2012). *Sexy girls, heroes and funny losers: Gender representations in children's TV around the world.* Peter Lang.
10 Soler, M.C., Kim, J. H., & Cecil, B. G. (2022). *Mapping internationalization on U.S. campuses: 2022 Edition.* American Council on Education.
11 For a selection of reviews and analyses, see, for example, Fahey, J., & Kenway, J. (2010). International academic mobility: Problematic and possible paradigms. *Discourse: Studies in the Cultural Politics of Education, 31*(5), 563–575; Kim, T. (2009). Shifting patterns of transnational academic mobility: A comparative and historical approach. *Comparative Education, 45*(3), 387–403; Kim, T. (2017). Academic mobility, transnational identity capital, and stratification under conditions of academic capitalism. *Higher Education, 73*(6), 981–997; Larner, W. (2015). Globalising knowledge networks: Universities, diaspora strategies, and academic intermediaries. *Geoforum, 59*, 197–205; Robertson, S. L. (2010). Critical response to Special Section: international academic mobility. *Discourse: Studies in the Cultural Politics of Education, 31*(5), 641–647.
12 Kim, T. (2010). Transnational academic mobility, knowledge, and identity capital. *Discourse: Studies in the Cultural Politics of Education, 31*(5). 577–591. See also other articles in that special issue.
13 Rizvi, F. (2005). Rethinking "brain drain" in the era of globalization. *Asia Pacific Journal of Education, 25*(2), 175–192.
14 Tzanakou, C., & Henderson, E. F. (2021). Stuck and sticky in mobile academia: Reconfiguring the im/mobility binary. *Higher Education, 82*, 685–693.

15 Burluk, O., & Rahbari, L. (2023). *Migrant academics' narratives of precarity and resilience in Europe.* OpenBook Publishers. https://doi.org/10.11647/OBP.0331.23; Guarnaccia, P. J. (2019). *Immigration, diversity and student journeys to higher education.* Peter Lang.
16 Kim, T. (2010). Transnational academic mobility, knowledge, and identity capital. *Discourse: Studies in the Cultural Politics of Education, 31*(5), 577–591; Qiongqiong, C., & Koyama, J. P. (2013). Reconceptualising diasporic intellectual networks: Mobile scholars in transnational space. *Globalisation, Societies and Education, 11*(1), 23–38.
17 Lane, J. (May 27, 2023). *On authenticity in ethnographic relationships and listening.* [Paper presented in a panel titled The meaning, study, and practice of authentic listening]. Annual Conference of the International Communication Association (ICA), Toronto, Canada.
18 Forsey, M. G. (2010). Ethnography as participant listening. *Ethnography, 11*(4), 558–572; see also The Center for Deep Listening. (n.d.) https://www.deeplistening.rpi.edu/deep-listening
19 Tobar, H. (2023). *Our migrant souls: A mediation on race and the meanings and myths of "Latino."* MCD/Farrar, Straus & Giroux.
20 Burluk, O., & Rahbari, L. (2023). *Migrant academics' narratives of precarity and resilience in Europe.* OpenBook Publishers. https://doi.org/10.11647/OBP.0331.23
21 Deterding, N. M., & Waters, M. C. (2018). Flexible coding of in-depth interviews. *Sociological Methods & Research, 50*(2), 708–739.

Chapter 2   The Seeds

1 Pollock, D., & Reken, R. (rev. ed., 2009). *Third culture kids: Growing among worlds.* Nicholas Brealey.
2 Pollock & Reken, *Third culture kids.*

Chapter 4   The Challenges

1 Elias, N., & Lemish, D. (2008). Media uses in immigrant families: Torn between "inward" and "outward" paths of integration. *International Communication Gazette, 70*(1), 21–40.
2 Pearce, R. (2016). Where are you from? *The International Schools Journal,* Athens, *36*(1), 18–26; Kebabi, A. (2024, pre-publication online). "'Where are you from?" and "foreigners." The discursive construction of identity in the personal everyday lives of well-established academics living in the UK. *Journal of Language and Discrimination, 8*(1), 100–120.
3 Katriel, T. (1986). *Talking straight: Dugri speech in Israeli Sabra culture.* Cambridge University Press.
4 Rings, G., & Rasinger, S. M. (2020). *The Cambridge handbook of intercultural communication.* Cambridge University Press.

5   See, for example, Meyers, M. (Ed.). (2012). *Women in higher education*. Hampton Press.
6   Bavishi, A., Madera, J. M., & Hebl, M. R. (2010). The effect of professor ethnicity and gender on student evaluations: Judged before met. *Journal of Diversity in Higher Education, 3*(4), 245–256; Chávez, K., & Mitchell, K.M.W. (2020). Exploring bias in student evaluations: Gender, race, and ethnicity. *Political Science & Politics, 53*(2), 270–274; Stoesz, B. M., De Jaeger, A. E., Quesnel, M., Bhojwani, D., & Los, R. (2022). Bias in student ratings of instruction: A systematic review of research from 2012 to 2021. *Canadian Journal of Educational Administration and Policy, 201*, 39–62.
7   See, for example, Reyes, V. (2022). Academic outsider: Stories of exclusion and hope. Stanford University Press; Sang, K.J.C., & Calvard, T. (2019). "I'm a migrant, but I'm the right sort of migrant": Hegemonic masculinity, whiteness, and intersectional privilege and (dis)advantage in migratory academic careers. *Gender Work Organ, 26*, 1506–1525.

Chapter 5   The Benefits

1   Kim, T. (2010). Transnational academic mobility, knowledge, and identity capital. *Discourse: Studies in the Cultural Politics of Education, 31*(5), 577–591; Kim, T. (2017). Academic mobility, transnational identity capital, and stratification under conditions of academic capitalism. *Higher Education, 73*(6), 981–997.
2   Simmel, G. ([1908]1950). "The Stranger." In *The Sociology of Georg Simmel* (K. H. Wolff, Trans.) (pp. 402–406). The Free Press. https://thebaffler.com/ancestors/stranger
3   Rogers, E. M. (1999). Georg Simmel's concept of the stranger and intercultural communication research. *Communication Theory, 9*(1), 58–74.
4   Larner, W. (2015). Globalising knowledge networks: Universities, diaspora strategies, and academic intermediaries. *Geoforum, 59*, 197–205.
5   Elias, N., & Lemish, D. (2008). Media uses in immigrant families: Torn between "inward" and "outward" paths of integration. *International Communication Gazette, 70*(1), 21–40.
6   Guarnaccia, P. J. (2019). *Immigration, diversity and student journeys to higher education*. Peter Lang.
7   Guarnaccia, *Immigration, Diversity and Student Journeys*.
8   S See, for example, Academic Freedom Alliance. https://institutionalneutrality.org/; Vasquez, M. (2024, February 9). Is institutional neutrality catching on? *ACTA in the News*, https://www.goacta.org/2024/02/is-institutional-neutrality-catching-on/; Kalven Committee: Report on the University's Role in Political and Social Action. https://provost.uchicago.edu/sites/default/files/documents/reports/KalvenRprt_0.pdf

9   Katriel, T. (1986). *Talking straight: Dugri speech in Israeli Sabra culture.* Cambridge University Press.
10 Henrich, J. (2020). *The WEIRDest people in the world: How the West became psychologically peculiar and particularly prosperous.* Farrar, Straus and Giroux; Henrich, J., Heine, S. J., & Norenzayan, A. (2010). The weirdest people in the world? *Behavioral and Brain Sciences, 33*(2–3), 61–83.
11 Arnett, J. J. (2008). The neglected 95%: Why American psychology needs to be less American. *American Psychologist, 63*(7), 602–614.
12 Lemish, D., & Jordan, A. (2022). Afterword: The invisible children, adolescents, and media and the future of our research. In D. Lemish (Ed.), *The Routledge international handbook of children, adolescents, and media* (pp. 514–516). Routledge.

Chapter 6   The Home

1   Mallett, S. (2004). Understanding home: A critical review of the literature. *The Sociological Review, 52*(1), 62–89.
2   Boocagni, P. (2017). *Migration and the search for home: Mapping domestic space in migrants' everyday lives.* Palgrave Macmillan.
3   Blunt, A., & Dowling, R. (2006). *Home.* Routledge.
4   Ahmed, S. (1999). Home and away: Narrative of migration and estrangement. *International Journal of Cultural Studies, 2*(3), 329–347.
5   Lems, A. (2020). Phenomenology of exclusion: Capturing the everyday thresholds of belonging. *Social Inclusion, 8*(4), 116–125.
6   See, for example, Aveling, N. (2001). 'Where do you come from?': Critical storytelling as a teaching strategy within the context of teacher education. *Discourse: Studies in the Cultural Politics of Education, 22*(1), 35–48; Hatoss, A. (2012). Where are you from? Identity construction and experiences of 'othering' in the narratives of Sudanese refugee-background Australians. *Discourse & Society, 23*(1), 47–68.
7   Glassman, J. (2009). Critical geographies 1: The question of internationalism. *Progress in Human Geography, 33*(5), 685–692.
8   Bhabha, H. K. (1994). *The location of culture.* Routledge.
9   Bhabha, *Location of culture.*
10 Blunt and Dowling, *Home*, Routledge.
11 These reflections were shared in an online project titled Quarantined across Borders. See also Ramasubramanian, S., Durham, A., & Cruz, J. (2022). Quarantined across borders: Theorizing embodied transnationalism, precarious citizenship, and resilience for collective healing. *Journal of Applied Communication Research, 50*(sup. 1), 53–39.
12 Hannerz, U. (1996). *Transnational connections: Cultures, people, places.* Routledge.
13 Easthome, H. (2004). A place called home. *Housing, theory and Society, 21*, 128–138.

14 Chen, Q., & Koyama, J. P. (2013). Reconceptualising diasporic intellectual networks: Mobile scholars in transnational space. *Globalisation, Societies and Education, 11*(1), 23–38.
15 Verghese, A. (2010). *Cutting for stone* (p. 95). Vintage Books.

Chapter 7   The Bridge

1 Abbots, E.-J. (2017). Approaches to food and migration: Rootedness, being and belonging. In J. A. Klein & J. L. Watson (Eds.), *The handbook of food and anthropology* (pp. 115–132). Bloomsbury; Varela, P. & Ares, G. (2017). Special issue: Food, emotions and food choice. *Food Research International, 76*(2), 179.
2 Anderson, B. (1983). *Imagined communities: Reflections on the origin and spread of nationalism.* Duke University Press.
3 Rushdie, S. (1991). *Imaginary homelands.* Granta Books.
4 Smets, K., Leurs, K., Georgiou, M., Witteborn, S., & Gajjala, R. (2020). *The Sage handbook of media and migration.* Sage.
5 Hegde, R. S. (2016). *Mediating migration.* Polity Press.
6 Lemish, D., & Elias, N. (2020). "We decided we don't want children. We will let them know tonight": Parental humor on social media in a time of the Coronavirus pandemic. *International Journal of Communication, 14*, 5261–5268.
7 Lemish, D., & Götz, M. (Eds.). (2007). *Children and media in times of war and conflict.* Hampton Press.
8 Hjorth, L. (April 22, 2021). Digital kinship—understanding intergenerational care at a distance. Keynote presented at the Migrant belongings: Digital practices and the everyday virtual conference. Utrecht University, The Netherlands.
9 Chouliaraki, L., & Georgiou, M. (2019). The digital border: Mobility beyond territorial and symbolic divides. *European Journal of Communication, 34*(6), 594–605.
10 Ponzanesi, S. (2019). Migration and mobility in a digital age: (Re)Mapping connectivity and belonging. *Television & New Media, 20*(6), 547–557.
11 Rushdie, S. (1991). *Imaginary homelands.* Granta Books.
12 Bhabha, H. K. (1994). *The location of culture.* Routledge.
13 Bhabha, *Location of culture*, p. 10.

Chapter 8   The Return

1 Rushdie, S. (1991). *Imaginary homelands.* Granta Books.
2 Remennick, L. (2022). No place like home: Sociocultural drivers of return migration among Israeli academic families. *Population, Space and Place, 28*(1), 1–12.

Chapter 9 The Support

1. Lemish, D., & Jordan, A. (2022). Afterword: The invisible children, adolescents, and media and the future of our research. In D. Lemish (Ed.), *The Routledge international handbook of children, adolescents, and media* (pp. 514–516). Routledge.
2. See discussion of feminist principles of journal editing, Lemish, D. (2021). Feminist editing of a mainstream journal: Reckoning with process and content related challenges. In S. Eckert & I. Bachmann (Eds.), *Reflections on feminist communication and media scholarship: Theory, method, impact* (pp. 16–29). Routledge.
3. Burluk, O., & Rahbari, L. (2023). *Migrant academics' narratives of precarity and resilience in Europe*. OpenBook Publishers. https://doi.org/10.11647/OBP.0331.23
4. Byerly, C. M. (2012). Gender, critical scholarship, and the politics of tenure and promotion. In M. Meyers, *Women in higher education: The fight for equity*. Hampton Press.
5. Thanks to Assistant Dean for DEI Bernadette Gilliard and the Rutgers Faculty Diversity Collaborative for calling my attention to this approach to mentorship. This item borrows some of the language from goals of their training material.
6. Other behavioral tips generally for inclusion and diversity that are immediately relevant to academic immigrants: Myers, V. A. (2013). *What if I say the wrong thing? 25 Habits for culturally effective people*. American Bar Association (ABA) Publishing.

Postscript

1. Feldman, N. (2024). *To be a Jew today: A new guide to God, Israel, and the Jewish People*. Farrar, Straus and Giroux.
2. Horn, D. (February 15, 2024). The return of the big lie: Anti-semitism is winning at Harvard and elsewhere, and old falsehood is capturing new minds. *The Atlantic*. https://www.theatlantic.com/ideas/archive/2024/02/jewish-anti-semitism-harvard-claudine-gay-zionism/677454/
3. hooks, b. (1995). *Killing rage: Ending racism* (p. 265). Holt.

Index

Page references in *italics* indicate a table.

academia: availability of resources, 42; balance between research and teaching, 43; financial benefits of, 40, 41, 44; gender inequality, 74, 75–76; as global enterprise, 105; graduate studies, 72–73; individualistic-competitive norms of, 72; marginalization of otherness in, 67–68, 82, 158; patriarchal elitism, 79; promotion procedures, 70; publishing in, 43–44; racism and discrimination in, 74–82, 166; relationships among colleagues, 68–69; relationships between professors and students, 71–73, 75; research opportunities in, 43–44; small talk in, 69; women of color in, 75, 119; work environment, 42
academic events, 161
academic fraudsters, 4
academic immigrants: adaptation processes, 57, 58; alienation of, 108; authority of, 70–71; career path, 4–5, 10, 41; as catalysts for change, 105; childhood experiences of, 20–21, 23–36; community-building opportunities, 162; contribution to institutional goals, 158; cosmopolitanism of, 8, 121, 122–123; cultural holidays and traditions, 160–161;

demographics of, 8, 10, *11*; detachment from place, 121; discomfort in the classroom, 100; double life of, 58–59, 159; employment status of, *11, 14–18*; evaluations of, 162; family background of, 25–28; fellowships, 57; gender and race of, *11, 14–18*; growing mobility of, 6–7; home and host countries of, 12–13, *14–18*; homecomings, 5–6; homeland news consumption, 134, 136–137, 138, 139–140; humor of, 100–101; identity conflicts, 9–10, 21, 73, 78–79, 119; institutional support of, 21–22, 156; integration into host society, 64, 116; intellectual impact of, 13, 85, 92–93, 158, 161–162; international students and, 162; interviews of, 9–11, 13, 18–19; leadership and interaction contributions, 102–105; linguistic skills and accents, 69–71, 160; lived experiences of, 7–8; marginalization of, 76, 84; marriage in host society, 38; mentorship by, 162–163; ongoing difficulties of, 63–67; otherness of, 21, 59, 162; personal sacrifices, 38; professional challenges of, 6, 67–82, 158–159; promotion of, 41, 42, 159, 162;

177

academic immigrants (cont.)
publication venues, 80; reappointment evaluations of, 159; recommendations about support of, 160–163; relationships with children and relatives, 9; relationships with students, 75; scholarly contributions, 4–5, 87–93; self-reflection of, 19, 31, 56–57; sense of loss, 114, 166; socializing habits, 82–83; solidarity among, 156–158; strategies for inclusion, 163; teaching contributions, 94–102; temporary jobs, 57; transformation of, 57; transitional challenges, 12, 21, 59–63, 162; travels of, 30–34; women, 75, 81–82, 119
academic mobility: cultural attitudes toward, 2–3, 52; patterns of, 8
academic nomads, 91
accents: communication difficulties and, 160; identity and, 70–71, 111, 116; immigrants' reactions to questions about, 108–109, 111; as markers of otherness, 107–108
Adorno, Theodore, 86
African knowledge, use of in pedagogical practices, 75–76, 96, 97
allegiance, 24, 115
ambience, 129, 135
American culture: interactional style, 66–67; irony and sarcasm, 64; lack of spontaneity, 64
"American Dream," 40
anti-Semitism, 65, 164, 165, 166–167
Arab knowledge, use of in pedagogical practices, 97–98
Arabs: assumptions about, 76
Arendt, Hannah, 86
Asians: care of elderly, 149; racial prejudice toward, 109
assimilation, 84, 112

Bauman, Zygmunt, 86
BBC, 35, 129
Belgium: political development in, 44; travel opportunities, 33

belonging: lived experience of, 112, 113, 124–125, 126–127, 129, 134
Bhabha, Homi, 121
Black Lives Matter movement, 102, 167
Black students, 73
Bolsonaro, Jair, 151
"brain drain," 7
"brain gain," 7
Brazil: cultural norms, 72; political turmoil in, 151
Brexit, 44–45, 115, 137, 139, 150–151
burial, 7, 123, 143, 144, 154

campus, 65, 75, 76, 159, 162, 164, 165
Canada: sense of identity, 116; social democracy in, 48
Catholic school, 29
challenges: in academia, 13, 67–69, 101, 157–159; of COVID-19, 123, 140; cultural, 63–67; financial, 26; of immigration, 2, 4, 85, 86; in interpersonal interaction, 69–71; linguistic, 21, 59, 69–71, 130, 131; professional, 6, 67–82, 158–159; of racism and discrimination, 73–82; of relationships with students, 71–73; of return to homeland, 143–144, 151; transitional, 6, 12, 21, 59–63, 162
childhood: immigration and, 23; importance of reading in, 35, 36; intellectual development and, 26; in mixed-cultural backgrounds, 27, 31, 32, 36; poverty and, 26, 27, 29; role of foreign languages in, 24, 31, 33; role of media in, 34–36; sense of "home," 31; travels in, 23–24, 30–33
China: political environment, 45–46; surveillance of academics in, 46; traditional festivals, 98
Chinese culture, sharing of in pedagogical practices, 97, 98
citizenship status, 114–115, 117
Civil Rights movement, 167
climate change movement, 123, 167

Colombia: employment opportunities, 41; sense of insecurity, 49
community: academic, 22, 124, 159; building of, 167; connections to food, 127, 128; COVID-19 and, 141; immigrant, 142, 162, 165; language and, 126, 131; networking and, 162; professional, 56
conflicts: in academia, 160; armed, 100, 140; between cultures, 120; Greek-Turkish, 46; of identity, 9–10, 21, 73, 78–79, 119; Israeli-Palestinian, 3, 4, 46, 76, 103, 157; as motivation for immigration, 12; political, 46, 159, 161; with students, 71
conversational style, 67, 103–104
cosmopolitan environments, 8, 25, 45, 115, 150, 151
COVID-19 pandemic: anti-Chinese attitudes during, 166; concept of home and, 123–124, 159; immigrants and, 140; media and, 140–141
culture codes, 64
culture shock, 60, 61, 63, 87
current events, 10, 21, 97, 101, 159, 161
Cutting for Stone (Verghese), 125
Cyprus, Greek-Turkish conflict in, 46

democracy, 3, 47, 48, 94, 153
Derrida, Jacques, 86
diasporas, 90, 142, 144, 165
"digital kinship," 141
digital newspapers, 136, 137
digital technologies, 141
disabilities, faculty with, 82, 159, 162
disasters, 12, 140, 159, 161
discrimination, 47, 59, 74, 75–76, 79, 80
diversity, equity, and inclusion (DEI) issues, 59, 87, 158, 159, 160, 161, 163
donors, 103, 104–105
double life, 58–59, 112–113, 146, 155, 159
dual identity, 112–113, 116, 118
dugri conversational style, 103
dying, 143–144, 154–155

economy, immigrant contribution to, 6, 7
education: parental devotion to, 29–31; value of, 24–25, 28–30, 36, 43
education bourgeoisie, 117
Einstein, Albert, 86
elderly relatives, 5, 61, 123, 140, 141, 143–145, 146, 148–149
employment: of academic immigrants, *11, 14–18*; COVID-19 and, 123; return to homeland and constraints of, 152
English language, 70, 71

family background: predisposition to immigration and, 25–26, 27–28, 32; value of education, 24–25, 26, 28–30, 36
feminism, 82
food: association with home, 127; community connections and, 128; cultural aspect of, 126–127; identity and, 127–128; sense of belonging and, 126–127
fragmented identity, 118, 121, 165
freedom: academic, 13, 44; political, 45; of the press, 96; of speech, 47, 151, 160; of thought, 122; to travel, 86
friends: in academia, 75, 95, 143; in the diaspora, 164–165; in the home country, 24, 93, 112, 116, 123, 126, 129, 134–135, 140, 144, 147, 161; in the host country, 52, 64, 66, 67, 133, 145; immigration and, 2, 38, 39, 41, 45, 46, 51, 52–53, 54, 57, 81, 111

Gandhi, Mahatma, 153
gays, 4, 5, 44
Gaza humanitarian crisis, 165
gender inequalities, 59, 74, 79, 82
geography, 25, 106, 140
German education, use of in pedagogical practices, 98
global citizenship, 121, 122–123, 124

graduate studies: change of plans during, 50–51; family matters and, 51; mentorship and support of, 52; as path for immigration, 49–50; visits to home country during, 50

Hall, Stuart, 86
health: mental, 4, 152; of parents, 149
health care: immigration and, 64, 123, 152; in Israel, 141
hegemonic culture, 118, 119
hegemonic White masculinity, 79, 172n7
higher education institutions: Diversity, Equity, and Inclusion (DEI) officers, 163, 164; internationalization of, 6–7; support of academic immigrants, 21–22
Hindu identity, 31, 98, 128, 153, 154
Historically Black Colleges and Universities, 73
historically marginalized groups, 163
home: absence of, 116–121; COVID-19 and, 123–124; definition of, 7–8, 12, 106–107, 111–112, 113, 123, 125; food and, 126; language and, 126; as place of safety, 123–124, 126; sense of loss of, 113–116; social relationships and, 107, 126; as a space, 107; in the world, 121–123
home country: changes in, 117; connection with relatives in, 143–144; definition of, 12; feeling of alienation from, 86, 116–121, 144–145, 151–152; vs. host country, 12; identity and, 107, 112–113; interest in current events in, 161; limitations of opportunities in, 53; media of, 133; movies and TV shows, 140; plans to return to, 50, 51, 143–144; sense of betrayal of, 40–41, 55–56; social networks, 147; studies of, 89–90; as true home, 111, 112, 115; visits to, 50, 117–119
"home-no-home" feeling, 120
"homing," process of, 106

hooks, bell, 167
host country: acceptance of, 145; adjustment to, 59; definition of, 12; engagement with politics and culture of, 139; vs. home country, 12; identity and, 112–113; marriage in, 38; sense of alienness in, 113–116, 120
hybrid identity, 141
hybrid liminal space in between cultures, 120

identity: crisis of, 114–115; detachment from, 121–122; food and, 127–128; homeland and, 112–113; immigration and, 9–10; intellectual, 121; maintenance of native, 110–111, 141–142; names and, 160. See also dual identity; fragmented identity; hybrid identity; national identity
identity politics, 119
illegal migrants, 12
imaginary homeland, 141–142
imagined communities, 129
immigrant children: adoption of host culture by, 132, 133; dual identity of, 142; passing of native language on, 131–132
immigrants: alienation of, 108, 113–114, 116; citizenship status, 114–115; connection to parents, 144–145, 146; cultural connections, 135–136; double lives of, 112–113, 146, 155; economic disparity, 88; identity crisis, 88, 114–115; integration into host country, 112, 116; interpersonal connections, 134–135; vs. migrants, 12; nostalgia of, 145; relations with children, 143; role of home country media in lives of, 6, 133–134; sense of belonging, 112, 113, 134, 167; sense of loss, 114, 142; sense of "otherness," 87, 88; stereotypes about, 76; transformation in self-perception, 51. See also academic immigrants

immigration: acceptance of, 37; as betrayal of the homeland, 40; challenges of, 2–3; emotional pressure, 54–55, 56; family reactions to, 52–53, 54–55, 56; friends reaction to, 53, 57; mini decisions about, 1–2; as "rite of passage," 40; self-identity explorations and, 89; studies of, 9–10, 157; university colleagues reaction to, 53–54. *See also* motivation for immigration
implicit racism, 82
in-between space, 120, 121, 122
India: communication studies in, 52; decline of democracy, 153; Hindu nationalism, 153; political development, 152–153
Indian identity, 98, 142
instant messaging platforms, 134–135
integration: into host society, 64, 112, 116, 124, 162; inward, 58; outward, 58, 59
intercultural communication, 89
International Communication Association (ICA), 11
international students, 7, 162
intersectionality issue, 81–82
inward integration, 58
Iran: experience of return to, 152; Islamic revolution in, 47; Western media's coverage of, 161
Islamophobia, 167
Israel: attitude to emigration, 2; decline of democracy in, 3; experience of returnees to, 147; Hamas war with, 78–79; health care system, 141; national identity, 40, 110–111, 118–119; post-Oslo development, 46; prejudice about, 77–78
Israel-Palestine relations, 164, 167

Japanese internment camps, 166
Jews: fragmented identity of, 165; Gaza humanitarian crisis and, 165; *vs.* Israelis, 166–167; lack of protection on campuses, 164; stereotypes of, 76–77; vilification of, 165; virtual networks, 165
journalism, 9, 11, 48, 95, 157, 161
Judaism, 166

labor, 13, 24, 103, 106, 129, 167
language education, 24, 31, 33–34. *See also* native language
Latina identity, 73, 75, 76, 80, 82
layered identity, 113
leadership at higher education institutions, 102, 103, 104
LGBTQ+ rights movement, 44, 47, 163, 167
literature, 20, 36, 89, 106, 125

Marcuse, Herbert, 86
marginalization, 67–68, 76, 82, 84, 158, 163
media: in childhood experiences, 34–36; erosion of trust in, 157; facilitation of cultural connections through, 135–136, 141; in life of immigrants, role of, 133–134, 141
"me-search" approach to scholarship, 89
motivation for immigration, 8–9, 21; children as, 38, 39; cultural expectation as, 40; family background as, 40; following a partner as, 37–38; following in the footsteps of siblings as, 39–40; graduate studies as, 49–52; looking for a fresh start as, 38–39; personal, 2, 37–40; political, 3, 44–49; professional, 3, 40–44
movies, 135–136
multicultural experience, 31, 36, 88, 122, 150
Muslim travel ban, 157

national identity, 121–122
national stereotypes, 115
nationalistic movements, 157

native language: in immigration experience, role of, 69–70, 130–132; as indicator of "home," 128; loss of, 129; passing on children, 130, 131–132, 133; sense of belonging and, 129; as source of security, 140
networking, 3, 58, 69, 83, 89, 92, 140, 147, 156, 159, 162, 164, 165
"new country." *See* host country
news from home country: consumption of, 136–137, 138, 139–140; disengagement from, 138–139; sources of, 136, 137
newspapers, 34

Obama, Barack, 3, 48–49
October 7, 2023, Hamas attack on Israel, 77, 120, 140, 157, 164, 166
otherness, 91, 94, 107–108
"outing" oneself as an outsider, 99
outsiders: feeling of being, 10, 64, 68, 84, 85, 87, 88, 90, 92, 97, 108, 113, 122–123, 158; in pedagogical practices, perspective of, 94, 99, 101–102
outward integration, 58, 59

Pakistan, social activism, 47
parents: care for elderly, 143–145, 146, 148–149; devotion to education, 29–31; immigrants' connection to, 144–145, 146; as role models, 30
patriarchal elitism, 79
pedagogical practices: comparative case studies, 96, 101; cross-cultural perspective in, 95, 97, 99–100; guest lectures, 97; humor in, 100–101; outsider perspective in, 94, 99, 101–102; sharing cultural traditions in, 98; sharing personal history in, 100
peer networks, 159
physical distance, 61, 115
politics: idea of return to homeland and, 146, 149–153; as motivation for immigration, 3, 44–49

Portugal: cultural norms, 72; prejudice against Brazilians, 74
privacy issue, 61
privileged opportunities, 11, 13, 40, 56, 57, 117, 122, 143, 166
promotion, 41, 42, 44, 70, 74, 78, 159, 162
Puerto Rican identity, 127–128
Puerto Rico: American attitude to, 114; pro-independence movement, 48; right-wing government in, 47–48

Rabin, Itzhak, 2
race relations, 65, 74, 79, 80, 83, 109, 110
racially minoritized faculty, 82
radio programs: as news source, 35, 136, 137
refugees, 27, 157, 161
resilience, 13, 81
resources: in academia, availability of, 42, 43, 58; peer networks, 159; for teaching, 95, 102
retirement, 146, 147–148, 152
return to homeland: to care for aging parents, 143–145, 146, 148–149; challenges of, 143–144, 151; end-of-life considerations, 154–155; financial and employment constraints of, 152; personal considerations of, 146, 147–149; political considerations of, 146, 149–153; relations with children and, 147–148, 154; retirement considerations, 152; sense of alienation after, 147
Romania: stereotypes about, 108–109
roots, cultural, 7, 40, 90, 92, 107, 119, 126, 130, 133, 136, 165
Rushdie, Salman, 142
Russian knowledge, in pedagogical practices, use of, 97
Rutgers University, 6

safety: feeling of, 107, 166; home as a place of, 123, 152
Said, Edward, 86

salary, 41, 74, 77
scholarship, 21, 86; immigrant passion for, 43, 87; new perspectives and approaches, 89, 90–92; personal motivations for, 93; research topics, 74, 88–90
self-identity explorations, 89
serendipity, 5, 50, 56, 57
sexism, 79, 153
Simmel, Georg, 85, 86
Six-Day War, 3
social connections, 63–64, 135–136, 141
staff, academic, 7, 29, 103
status: of employment, 11, 18; immigrant, 12, 13, 100, 104, 114, 116, 122, 149
stereotyping, 76–77, 95, 108–109, 110, 111, 114
stranger, concept of, 85–86
students: backgrounds, 100; ignorance about foreign cultures, 75–76; interactions with faculty, 71–73, 94, 95

"taken for granted" social phenomenon, 85
teaching. *See* pedagogical practices
television shows, 35, 135–136
Thatcher, Margaret, 45
"third culture kids," 31, 32
Third Space, 120, 141, 167
Tiananmen Square massacre, 45
Tikkun Olam tradition, 167
transition: to another country, challenges, 6, 12, 21, 37, 50, 56, 59–63, 76, 106, 162; to another identity, 118
transnational "strangers," 86
travels: in childhood, 23–24, 30–33; language education and, 33–34; for political reasons, 32; for vacations and family visits, 32–33, 34
Tree of Life synagogue shooting, 157
Trump, Donald, 56, 150, 157

United Kingdom: citizenship, 151; criticism of Israel, 77; political development, 44–45, 150–151
United States: anti-Semitism in, 65, 164; Canadian view of, 41, 56; European view of, 38; exceptionalism of, 48; fragmented society, 152; freedoms of, 151; gun laws, 65; political development in, 64–65, 150; race relations, 65; religion in, 62; safety, 153; struggle for academic freedom, 160. *See also* American culture
universality, 105, 157

Verghese, Abraham: *Cutting for Stone*, 125

"Wandering Scholar," concept of, 8, 12
WEIRD (Western, Educated, Industrialized, Rich, Democratic) dominance of academia, 105, 157
WhatsApp, 134, 135, 164, 165
"Where are you from" exchanges, 107, 108, 110, 111, 116
White identity, 99, 114, 119
White masculinity, 79, 80
women, as academic immigrants, 75, 81–82, 119
work connections, 63–64

Xi Jinping, 46

Zionism, 51, 165, 166–167

About the Author

DAFNA LEMISH is a Distinguished Professor and Interim Dean of the School of Communication and Information at Rutgers University. She is a prolific scholar of children, gender, and media, a fellow of the International Communication Association, and the founding editor of the *Journal of Children and Media*.